Parkinson's Blues

Stories of My Life

Parkinson's Blues

Stories of My Life

John J. Clayton

Paragon House
Saint Paul

First Edition 2020

Published in the United States by
Paragon House
St. Paul, Minnesota

www.ParagonHouse.com

Cover design by Ella Gold

Library of Congress Cataloging-in-Publication Data

Names: Clayton, John Jacob, author.

Title: Parkinson's blues : stories of my life / John J. Clayton.
Description: First edition. | Saint Paul : Paragon House, 2020. | Summary: "This book begins describing the onset of Parkinson's, the arrival of the dark unexpected. In a Monty Python skit, someone is nagged by questions. "I didn't expect the Spanish Inquisition," he complains. Suddenly Michael Palin, in red 16th century costume, bursts into the room. "Nobody expects the Spanish Inquisition!" he shrieks. Who expects the onset of Parkinson's? Or cancer? Or stroke? Or the loss of a child?
The terrible surprise isn't limited to Parkinson's. It's the existential condition of everyone's life. In fourteen sketches, John J. Clayton links the experience of PD with the experience of childhood sickness, family battles, the struggle to make a good life out of a painful life"-- Provided by publisher.

Identifiers: LCCN 2020005230 (print) | LCCN 2020005231 (ebook) | ISBN 9781557789433 (paperback) | ISBN 9781610831253 (ebook)
Subjects: LCSH: Clayton, John Jacob. | Clayton, John Jacob--Health. | Authors, American--20th century--Biography. | Parkinson's disease--Patients--United States--Biography.
Classification: LCC PS3553.L388 Z46 2020 (print) | LCC PS3553.L388 (ebook) | DDC 813/.54 [B]--dc23
LC record available at https://lccn.loc.gov/2020005230
LC ebook record available at https://lccn.loc.gov/2020005231

Manufactured in the United States of America

10 9 8 7 6 5 4 3 2 1

The paper used in this publication meets the minimum requirements of American National Standard for Information Sciences—Permanence of Paper for Printed Library Materials, ANSIZ39.48-1984.

For Laura and Steven

Contents

Parkinson's Blues 1

Congregation of the Broken 15

Good Blood 31

Energy 37

How to Heal Parkinson's 49

The Angry Bear 59

Fantasies of Disaster 67

Radical Hero 73

A Nervous Stomach 89

The Aunts 99

Waiting for Polly Adler 115

Josh 135

A Broken Compass 145

Coda: A Mystery 153

ONE

Parkinson's Blues

HERE'S WHAT I THOUGHT was in store for me as I grew old:

I'd stay clear, strong and energized through my eighties, keep writing stories, and then I'd slow down and my heart would begin to give out, a stammering motor catching, stumbling, dimming—sunlight blocked by cloud—and there'd be a time when I'd say goodbye, goodbye to wife and children and friends, and then rational consciousness would slip away, I'd fade into oblivion or, better, be enfolded into radiance, the radiance that emanates through all the worlds, and I, barely *I* anymore, would feel the diffusion of my individual light as it spread and spread.

But no, it turns out, no, that's not what's in store. For in my early eighties Parkinson's has settled on me, a vulture. It followed upon a terrible case of shingles. There's no cure. This is the beginning. The Parkinson's won't kill me—I keep getting told this, as if it should comfort me. It won't kill me—but it has already submerged my life.

I shake, I tremble. I have a hard time swallowing. So I drool. Have begun to stumble. Ah, but that's the least of it. Worse, I become exhausted, wake exhausted, nap often. I'm usually half asleep. If I take a pill, I can obtain an hour of writing—slow, muddy writing on my laptop.

And maybe still worse, when I speak with friends or in a group—a book group, a political group—it often feels as if my brain is under water. Everything slows, slows. I reach for an idea, like a stutterer reaching for a word, struggling to enunciate a word, but it has disappeared. My mind feels sluggish, thick, yet empty, blank. There's silence in the room. The group, uncomfortable but wanting to help, waits, kindly giving me time. I can feel their encouragement. I finally come up with a reduced version of my idea, lacking specifics, spoken in a guttural croaking. A frog speaks.

All my adult life I've had the ability to manipulate categories, play with the nuances of texts. Now I'm afraid, and with good reason, that I'll have nothing to say. If I write down an idea, I'm able to read it aloud and speak with the old intelligence. But I forget the names of scholars, the titles of books or films. My analytical abilities, my understanding, remain. For now. But I've become unsure about everything. Have I been punished because I've been intellectually arrogant? Paid back for being a fool? I don't believe the world works that way—that God works that way. But who knows how the world works? How God works?

Though worms destroy my body,

yet in my flesh shall I see God.

What can that mean?

My body is already being destroyed.

Early one morning I stop in the middle of morning prayers, and in a moment of insight—or perhaps its opposite, delusion—decide that, in a sense, I'm in a place I've never heard anyone describe: both alive and not alive. Like a ghost, I can look from a distance upon my children, my wife, our friends—and love those I look upon. For a year or—God forbid—*ten* years, I'll be an observer ghost. Standing far outside, above the living world, but not hiding away in shame. I'll still visit my children, I'll still eat—though ghosts don't eat so very much—still cook with pleasure, still read books, though not so fluently, and I forget what I've read; maybe I'll even write stories, as I've done all my life, though now with more difficulty than I've ever faced. But secretly, inwardly, I'll be separate, taking in the world without acting in it.

It's foolish to strive. Saul Bellow's Augie March tells us, *when striving stops, the truth comes as a gift.* A ghost's truth: nothing at stake. I offer no resistance, claim nothing, and take no solid position. I let the food fall off my fork. I cope on my own. Ghosts don't join together for mutual support. My entire adult life I've been firm, if anything, too firm. Now I'm permeable. Nothing to battle against, no expectation of a miracle cure, and if you're lucky it gets worse more slowly. Some joke.

I exercise hard, I stretch. I take time to notice and to love—maybe because as a ghost I don't put myself in the way. I love more, not less. My love surprises me. I sleep badly, and there are mornings when I groan and grumble—not a well-behaved ghost. By noon I'm usually in the mode of ghostly acceptance.

I don't expect a lot, and my friends and family don't expect a lot from me. I wonder if they see the love since my face has stiffened, I'm told, into a "mask": the frozen face of Parkinson's. I never expected to have a frozen face. With effort, I can smile fully, with eyes and cheeks and mouth. But as a ghost I prefer not to make the effort. To do so feels dishonest, like modeling for a camera.

A ghost? But please! Who do I think I'm kidding? Some ghost! Do ghosts drool? Does food get stuck in their throat? Oh, I'd like to talk myself into seeing my disease not as deterioration but as an opportunity for spiritual growth. But isn't it self-deception to pretend I'm lucky to stumble along on Parkinson's? How lucky is it to watch food tremble off my fork? Foolish to strive? It's striving just to get myself up in the morning. I'm no ghost. To meditate in morning prayer is a struggle. I strap on tefillin and mumble words of gratitude and awe and try to feel connected with the One. But fatigue fills me. I've always believed that you find your deepest life not by getting rid of difficulties, not by asking everything to go smoothly, but by sailing your hard ship through difficult seas. The seas will change you, will make you a sailor. And now? And now?

I mug at myself in a mirror, recite Monty Python's running gag. In the middle of a skit in which a character complains at being questioned, saying as hyperbole, "I didn't expect a kind of Spanish Inquisition," in bursts Michael Palin in Sixteenth Century red cape, and sneers, "*Nobody expects the Spanish Inquisition.*"

***

I don't want to lie to myself, but, knowing there's no cure, I look for a scrap of good to come not in spite of but *through* this diminishment. What an odd experience, to find in myself a flabbiness of spirit, a lack of desire. *Abulia.* Will-less-ness: maybe the opposite of *ebullience*. The only motives I can count on, in the midst of lethargy and apathy—this abulia—are the desire to desire, and the guilt that I lack desire. All the energy I've had throughout my life, and now, so little. Sometimes I sit at my desk just looking into space while torpor and self-pity fill me.

I'm ashamed that I've never been sufficiently filled with gratitude for my energy—for my breath, for the ability to read, to talk, to write. What remains? I find that I've become more aware of the warmth of the sun on my face, of trees swaying, shimmering with a delicate, incipient green after the first spring greening rain, more aware of the reds and the gold of deep autumn. And what about my love for my wife and my children? Oh, that remains.

Not just *remains*; it grows, and for that I'm grateful.

Every morning my first prayer, *Modeh ani,* offers thanks to God for awakening my soul once again; *I give thanks before You . . . . Great is Your faithfulness.* Awakening my body out of the dark of sleep; awakening my spirit to the things of this world, things that, seen in a holy light, become holy.

I can walk, thank God. Every long stride feels like a victory. And I can see, I can hear. But more easily I focus on the damage; gratitude is something I have to manufacture—it doesn't come without effort. Is this gratitude a way of deceiving myself, a way of pretending to compensate for what's lost, broken? Broken and irreparable. There are ways of holding back the growth of symptoms: exercises for developing balance and strength. And what about the pills meant to make up for the loss of dopamine, or pills that give a temporary shot of energy? They work a little—until they don't. There's no way I can fight my way back to clarity of mind and full wakefulness. The more I fight the less good I'll take from this. Any victory of spirit has to come from not whining and not struggling.

I feel like an old man, wanting to stay comfortable till I die, yet knowing that unless I give myself up to the unknown I might as well die right now. How am I going to make use of this time? That's not the right question. To say "make use of" is to think you're in control, but I need to relinquish control. Will the tremors increase and spread to the rest of my body? Will my mind's viscosity, its sluggishness, increase? Will my mind be more and more submerged?

***

I was riding the trolley—a *streetcar* we called it—down Broadway, upper West Side, from my classes at Columbia College, riding the old Broadway trolley—so you can imagine how long ago this was—the 1950s, when there were still trolleys in Manhattan. Rocking cross street to cross street, it jingled to warn cars crossing the tracks. I remember a sunny day. The afternoon sun going down over the other side of the Hudson slanted on every block between the buildings. I sat on a hard rattan seat looking down at my book as we jogged along.

I wasn't paying attention. What I tell you about the sun or about the stiff rattan seats is true; but frankly, I have to reconstruct it after the fact. I was oblivious then.

I began to be aware of a conversation going on next to me. A distinguished older man in jacket and tie was exchanging words with a well-dressed woman, same age, maybe sixty, maybe seventy. He tipped his fedora and stood up, she sat down in his place, and they commenced to talk about the "younger generation." To talk about *me*— isn't it a shame, young people nowadays.

Do they think to give you a seat? How were they brought up?

They just sit—just sit and watch you stand.

They must think they're privileged.

They spoke loudly, so I would hear and take shame.

Not fair! I had been in the world of my book. Usually, in fact, I made it a point to offer my seat to a lady or an old man.

Nevertheless, I swallowed the shame and carried it block after block as the elderly gentleman and the elderly lady entertained themselves talking about me. If I'd been older, I'd have entered the conversation, laughed at my own impoliteness, and apologized. But I'd waited too long and was too young and too mortified. They were old—white hair and wrinkles, probably full of aches and pains.

I waited for my stop at 86th Street. I didn't really plan my strategy; it came to me as I put the book in my book bag. As the streetcar slowed, I got up and, blank of face, I played the gimp, the poor cripple, played it as if I were trying to avoid playing it, limping, limping, limping down the aisle, not looking back, careful not to exaggerate, one shoulder just a little higher than the other, grasping seat backs and poles, and then, when the door opened, I made my painful way down the steps and out the trolley. When I crossed to the sidewalk, I kept limping till the streetcar was well down the tracks so that if they saw me, the old people, even a block away, they'd see a cripple, a poor crippled boy that they'd bad-mouthed. Let them, the old man and the old woman, take on the embarrassment, the moral self-condemnation! What will they say to each other? What can they say?

I was elated.

Now it's more than sixty years later. I think about my struggle with Parkinson's. You, my wife, you've been so good to me, but we both know it's not going to get better. That's the way it is. I'm not yet gimping or shuffling, not yet. I can imagine walking down the aisle not of a trolley but of a rocking subway or a bus, slightly blank of face from the Parkinson's; stiff, and needing to hold on. And those old people, long dead, watch me walk. Ghosts. Not so funny now, is it, one of them says.

They have the last laugh.

***

I know, my wife, you've had enough of this groaning and of having to pity me.

"Not pity," you say, "not pity, sweetheart. Is that all you've learned? Suppose," you say, "you'd died at forty. All right, you might have had fewer wrinkles and fewer aches and pains, but you'd have done so much less in the world. You'd have felt so much less, been so much less a person." And you laugh, "At forty, you wouldn't even have met me."

Well, it's true. I kiss your cheek, my beauty, submitting to what you say. Love can be a distillate of growing old; and I've loved you more and more, loved the children more and more. Yes, we deepen. But oh, my God, what we pay for the deepening.

I pray for equanimity. I want to acknowledge my sickness with equanimity. But I don't want to lie. This long diminishment may, I pray, be a blessing. The trivial is discarded, shrugged off; the ordinary and everyday accrue meaning, even beauty. It's not just the Spanish Inquisition that's not expected. God is here, woven into the contradictions. Into the gap that takes the breath away.

***

Who expects life in the form it arrives? The Spanish Inquisitor knocks at the door. All my life he's been waiting to burst in. Who knew? Now the inquisitor enters with his case full of instruments; this is going to be the story of the rest of my life. What's to do about it?

Funny as a crutch the way our lives turn out. You'll die laughing.

It's three o'clock in the morning. Aches and pains have replaced sleep. My right calf wakes me in nasty spasm. At the same time, because my throat constricts from the Parkinson's, I have to squeeze my swallow to get down the pills I take for Mr. Parkinson, pills for said aches and pains.

"Said aches & pains;" I hear my language trying to make this a laughing matter, or make my own groaning a laughing matter. As if words could change things. I sigh; I watch my fingers shake. I offer up a couple of deep groans: *Oi*!

That *oi* of Yiddishkeit tries to handle pain with humor. I laugh at myself, as if to say, *Whadaya think, chump? You expect the physical laws of the universe to be revoked just for you? What chutzpah!* But how funny is it, somebody tell me, please, how funny when you have to descend the stairs right foot down to the next step, left plays catch up, right foot down again? It's no laughing matter, as my mother used to say.

Still, this *oi,* this mode of handling suffering can maybe be a little funny, something of a help. Why? Because implied self-deprecation sets you slightly apart from the pains. You split yourself, make fun of the complainer, though the complainer is you. And the word, *pains,* the plural, makes light—as against the singular, *pain.* Pains can be funny; pain can't. *Funny as a crutch.*

From one to ten, how much pain are we dealing with here? Not a lot. Nothing to do with the Parkinson's. Let's call it a five point three, ladies and gentlemen. Aach. Not so terrible; but not all that funny. And now, three-fifteen in the morning, the cramp melts, the calf relaxes, and the old guy can stumble out of bed, foot to the floor, other foot to the floor, can he stick the landing?—and yes! Yes, he can. Let's give said old guy a round of applause.

Uncertain legs carry me to 3 A.M. bathroom, back to bed again, where my wife Sharon stirs.

"You okay?" she murmurs. "What's the matter?"

"Who said anything's the matter?"

"You groaned. Goodnight, then," she says, and turns over, already asleep. Her sleep comforts my wakefulness. And I keep vigil till the morning light makes distinct the dresser, the bedside tables, my slippers under the window. Once I get myself up for the day and exercise for the better part of an hour, and my pills have had time to work

— time for the pain, deep sluggishness, and exhaustion to diminish, time for the tremors to quiet, I've got it beat for the morning. Later, I'll stride the treadmill.

My job now is to keep Parkinson's from becoming the totality of my day.

Have you ever seen a three-legged dog walking free or on a leash, trotting sprightly on three legs? Maybe one leg lost to a truck. While the surgery is healing, he may whine for pain, kept from licking at the wound by an uncomfortable lampshade collar, but once the wound heals and the collar's off, he adjusts to the new condition as if there were no loss—*it's the way I am.* Does he miss the leg? It doesn't seem so. A dog will mourn for a lost master or for the loss of another dog in the same household, but not for a lost leg. He doesn't seem to experience the contrast between now and before.

Let me become like a three-legged dog.

What should I make of this life? I make, have always made, words.

I'd like to be brave, like to be cavalier—at least pretend to myself to be cavalier. But again and again I fall into monitoring my losses and my potential losses, as if I were a banker of myself. It's a bum investment. I might as well live it up, turn spendthrift, prodigal, profligate.

Very nice, very nice. See if you can fool yourself with words.

We all know the way we're supposed to respond to a sickness such as Parkinson's. So that at the memorial service a eulogy can say, "He fought his sickness, but he never complained. He was kind and generous. He expressed gratitude for the life given him." I'm not going to lie in order to rate a decent eulogy. I don't want to lie to myself, to fake it.

Dear God, help me accept what's coming to me. Help me join what's coming as to the strange music of a dance. I want to dance to the new music. You, coming through the ballroom door, teach me to dance. Be my partner in the dance.

TWO

Congregation of the Broken

I'VE NEVER SEEN him here before. A fat man, obese, a man in his sixties, sits beside me in synagogue. It's a Shabbat morning service. Flab swells his cheeks, belly sags and thighs bulge. Under a tallis, his jacket is open, his white shirt tight at the buttons; he must have gained weight since he bought it. I'd move to another seat to give his bulk room to spread, but I don't want to embarrass him. He gives off warmth and a mild acrid odor—I don't much mind, but the warmth and the odor express, somehow, the sadness of the man or my sadness in seeing him.

While our young rabbi is chanting opening prayers, the fat man murmurs along. He seems familiar with the prayers, but not knowing the protocol of this synagogue, doesn't realize that the prayer book is in a compartment under the seat in front of him. Before I have a chance to point it out, he lifts himself, great beast, and straining, stiff, walks up the aisle to take a prayer book from a cart of extras by the door, now lumbers back to his seat, burdened by his extra hundred or more pounds, and burdened, too, I imagine, by all the eyes he thinks are watching him.

Or am I inventing this self-consciousness? Does he really feel everyone is watching, or is that my fantasy? As he sits down again beside me, I lean over, whisper the page number. He nods, he opens the prayer book, finds his place. I feel a connection with him, a common sorrow; an understanding washes over me, as it does often these days: it's not just me, not just him, it's all of us: we're a congregation of the broken and the disappointed. We want others to see us as whole, undamaged, perfect. We're not perfect.

I feel that especially, I suppose, because I've been struck with Parkinson's, and it leaves me ragged. Sometimes it feels like the end of my life. I'm not alone. Across the aisle, Saul, another congregant with Parkinson's—helped by his wife—shuffles into a seat a few rows down. The condition came upon him twenty years ago; he has a much more advanced case. If I live that long, I'll move to a next stage, and a next.

Parkinson's is an excellent teacher. You thought you were special? Think again. Before the Parkinson's, when I'd see those who are manifestly imperfect—the crippled, the addicted, the mad—I kept them at a distance: *Thank God I'm not like him, not like her.* I felt pity; I felt distaste. Walking on a downtown street past damaged people, broken people, I'd wince.

Fool, I say to myself now—to act as if only the lame or blind or schizophrenic were broken. All of us broken, we pass one another in the aisle of a supermarket; we sit together in a doctor's waiting room or in synagogue. Passing on a downtown sidewalk by a young man in torn jeans talking to himself, shaking his head, I said the appropriate blessing: *Blessed are You, Lord our God, who makes creatures so various.* Did I believe in the blessing? Or did I say the words to keep my own brokenness at bay?

Wearing the frozen mask of Parkinson's, I no longer have the privilege of keeping my brokenness hidden. That's all to the good, I tell myself. It's a peculiar benefit of my condition that I can't pretend to be perfect, to have it together, to be special, in a world of the broken. All of us broken.

Many in this congregation, I know, have gone through treatment for cancer. Elise, two rows down, wears a scarf to hide loss of hair from radiation. Across the room is a man I know, not by name, recovering from a stroke; his walker waits folded at the end of the row. Near the entrance at the side of the sanctuary, there's Donna, blind, her service dog at her feet. But it's not just brokenness in the body I'm thinking of. I'm thinking of the masks we wear, even in synagogue, to disguise our imperfections. I'm thinking of the way we hold our heads, our false smiles; the way, pretending to be perfect, we stay separate from others with a look of judgment or pity—pity often a disguised form of judgment.

Still, it feels soothing to be here in synagogue. Many of us see one another almost every Saturday morning. For a few hours, perhaps, we forget our singularity, our uniqueness. During the week we may imagine ourselves as special—special sufferers, special victims who don't deserve to suffer—while in fact we're ordinary people, trying to paste over the cracks in the masks we wear. The Shabbat service helps us see through quiet eyes.

But even in synagogue, cracks are visible.

A paradox: keeping the core of ourselves hidden, lest it reveal that we're not special, that we're broken, we display a cracked mask that reveals the very damage we're trying to hide. We design masks; we tell ourselves stories, to hide the damage or to excuse ourselves. But sometimes we can look through the mask, deep in, to where soul breathes. And the mask, the story, they aren't only devices to keep the damage at bay; they can also be beautiful in their own right.

***

He wears baggy trousers, chinos held up, like a clown's, with suspenders. The fat man, wrinkled, balloons out under a jacket that once belonged to a suit. I'm guessing he can no longer wear the trousers. He breathes laboriously; how hard his heart must have to work. "We're up to the *Barechu*," I whisper. The teacher in me tells him, "It's not a prayer for individuals but for all of us as a community." The man nods. Does he already understand without me? I point, silently, to the Hebrew and to the

English translation. I leave him be.

***

"My darling," my mother used to say, "Do you know how special you are? No, really. But of course, why shouldn't you be, with me as your mother?"

Special. When I say the word, an image of my mother comes into my head, an image from almost half a century ago. My mother stands beside me—I'm in my thirties, she's in her seventies—in the lobby of the residential hotel on Central Park West where she spent her last few years after my father died. "Look at them," she half-whispered, that Bette Davis drawl of hers hoarsened by so many cigarettes. She pointed with her cane at one old man, then another, leaving the lobby, and whispered, "They're *old*, look at them, *so* old! I'm not old like *that*, am I?" She pinched my arm through my shirt sleeve. "*Am* I?"

No, no, I assure her as I was expected to assure her, "Old? You're not old," I told her. "You're still beautiful. You'll never get old. In fact," I laugh, "I'm older than you—which is quite a feat. You're some amazing woman."

"You're joking, I suppose, you think it's charming, making fun of your poor mother, I know. But isn't it true, my darling? Really—or do you think I'm *ordinaire* and old?"

"No. No. In your heart," I comforted, "you're as young as the day you came to this city. I really think so. Little girl from Russia, young woman from Rochester. I'm not kidding you, Mom."

This satisfied her for a while. She sighed and began her essential narrative. "I am a little bit special," she said, smiling, lifting her voice, thrilled by her own voice. "I came to New York with no money. *Keine gelt.* But," she said, tapping my shoe with the tip of her cane so I'd pay attention, "I had a connection to old man Bonwit—I've told you—of Bonwit Teller. He could see what I was—a *très* unusual woman. I made him laugh! And *I* knew what women wanted in clothing. I had an instinct. In a year I was his coat buyer. Not so bad, wouldn't you say? I was sent to Paris in the spring to sketch the latest fashions—yes, my son, I know I've told you all this a thousand times. Indulge me, *mon cher.* What have I got but my memories? . . . And in the evening—in New York or in Paris—I was taken by this man or that man to the theater or to a splendid party. Several times I was at a party with Al Jolson. Look how far I came! A little immigrant child. But then. . . then I met your father," she sighed. "And I fell in love. Do me something! Now, don't get me wrong. A wonderful man, your father, may he rest in peace. But. . ." She sighed again. "It's not entirely his fault. His charmer of a brother, your uncle, ruined his life."

Over and over, this story. Frozen, obsessive, becoming the shape of a life. Not just my mother's, my father's, but my own.

"Your father has never been sick a day in his life," my mother used to say— half jealous, half celebrating his strength. She was sick every day with heartburn, drank boiled water for relief. She sighed, she groaned. And me, I was sick with headaches and stomach aches when my father was away in California taking care of his father—and sick when he came home and we met him at the train, though each time he returned I was full of love and excitement. By the time we left Grand Central, we were each angry at one another, caught up in the same old story of victim/victimizer; he criticized what?—the stain on my shirt, the length of my hair. I pulled away and wouldn't talk to him—and I'd brew a headache.

My father went to work day in, day out, never taking a vacation, never taking a sick day. I was afraid that if he saw me sick, he'd tell me not to be a baby. I waited for him to leave in the morning before I got out of bed. Then I'd call out, "Mom? I think maybe I have a temperature."

Dad worked for his brother Lloyd—his younger brother, whom my mother referred to as the "big shot." The special one. How she hated and envied Lloyd. He had established himself selling tires—he had cards printed: *WORLD'S LARGEST DISTRIBUTOR,* though in fact when he started the business, he had no tires at all, just a one-room office off 11th Avenue. He'd travel through the Northeast, sleeping on trains, sleeping coach, to avoid spending on hotels, taking money from gas stations for promised tires, then going to Akron or Dayton to put in orders for seconds. He loved to say, "In those days I worked twenty-five hours a day eight days a week." By the time I was born he was rich.

My father had been a shoe salesman in Chicago. Lloyd convinced him to come into the business in New York. He needed someone he could trust. According to my mother, they were supposed to be equal partners, but Lloyd created a new company and bullied my father into signing away his rights.

My mother begged my father to leave him. They fought about this all the time. "Why do you stay with a man like that when you could go in fifty-fifty with Jimmy Martin? How can you call it loyalty when you're slaving—with no recognition, no money—for a sonofabitch like Lloyd?"

Then there were times she sympathized. "Your poor father, he means well, but he's so afraid of his brother. I've said that your father is never sick, but his fear, that's his sickness. His fear! He lets that man run over him."

And I guess it was true. I remember when I was a young boy, in the 1940s, how afraid my father was of Lloyd's temper, of his cold-eye judgment. Before we'd visit my uncle at the office, maybe once or twice a year, Dad made sure I had a haircut and dressed me up, found a stain and made me change my shirt, and on the way downtown in the subway he'd spit on his handkerchief and scrub my face one last time.

"The big guy ready for us?" he'd ask the receptionist. Then he'd clear his throat, my father, put on a big grin, and knock at his brother's door.

Sometimes Uncle Lloyd was expansive and charming,

a grandiose narcissist. Sitting at his oversized mahogany desk—it must have weighed three hundred pounds, that desk—he'd teach me about money, philosophize about responsibility, then call for his car and a tire changer would have it running at the warehouse door. And he'd pat the car and open the door for us and say, "How d'you like this beat-up old cigar box I bought last week, Jackie?"—always his name for me—and jam his foot down on the accelerator and the new Caddy would spring forward, jamming us back into the plush seats. He'd park the car where he pleased, leaving a card from the police chief on his dashboard. We'd go eat at Lindy's, where he palmed the headwaiter a tip and we sat with "the big shots."

"See that guy over there? That's Jimmy Durante," he'd say, his lips unmoving like a movie gangster's. "Jimmy Durante. The Schnoz." And he'd wave the waiter over for more pickles. When my father wasn't looking or was pretending not to look, Lloyd would jam a ten-dollar bill into the handkerchief pocket of my jacket.

Other times he'd be in a lousy mood—yelling at one of his salesmen, at his secretary, at a tire changer. He'd kick his way through the aisle at piles of tires and snap at my father, "Get that crap cleaned up, will you? What kind of shit hole you want to work in, Chuck?"

"You bet, Lloyd. I'll have them get right on it!" And, his beefy face hot, red, my father would storm back to the huge warehouse and roar, "Danny! Goddamnit—you get the hell in here!"

By the time I was in high school, my father was more Lloyd's gofer than a chief salesman. He still leased tires to a number of taxi fleets and ran the parking lot and sold tires, but he spent a lot of time driving Lloyd to the dentist or the barber's and coming back for him later.

Lloyd was the special one in the family.

My father would never have called himself special. To be special was to be a phony, "like your dear mother," or a big shot "like my rich brother." Dad thought of himself as a plain American and a "regular guy"—not a "furriner": an Italian or German or Irish or Eastern European or a black or even a Jew—though he was born a Jew. All the ethnic hyphenates he called by their derogatory slang names. He also had it in for professors or musicians (long-hairs) or artists (phonies) or the fancy rich or commies or homos.

We lived on the seventh floor of an apartment building on West 84th Street. A couple of times as we were taking the elevator down, if it stopped and the door opened on the sixth floor, and Mr. B—a refugee from Hitler—was taking his dog down for a walk, my father would yell, "Take the next trip. I don't need no goddamn dogs riding with me." The elevator door shut, leaving the man and his dog. My father poked me and whispered, "Also, we don't need no damn furriners." He grinned at me, wanting to get my approval. "We showed him, didn't we?" I was ashamed of him, and my father knew it, and knew my mother was also ashamed of him.

Now I see what made me notice the stranger sitting beside me. He looks more than a little like my poor, overweight father—though this stranger is much heavier, and though I suspect that, unlike my father, this man has been to services before.

My father went to synagogue only once in his life—the day I became Bar Mitzvah—and even then, my mother had to shame him into coming.

He didn't want to spend money on my "getting a bar mitzvah"—*getting,* like getting a haircut—but my mother put her foot down. She wouldn't talk to him, wouldn't say a word, until he agreed. She let him vent—*how stupid, what's the boy need that for? You think I'm made of money?* But in the end, he let her make arrangements. She hired a rabbinical student to teach me. I learned the chanting by rote, understanding almost nothing. As an adult, I've had to learn from scratch.

On the day I became *Bar Mitzvah,* my father came to synagogue for my chanting of the Haftarah. With the encouragement of the rabbi, he went up to the bima, where the Torah scroll was laid open on a slanted table, and he read—in transliteration—the blessing of the Torah. He'd practiced the "mumbo jumbo" the night before.

Stepping down after the blessing, sitting beside me, grinning, he whispered, "How you like that? I bet the rabbi thought I was reading the Hebrew. You think? Think I fooled him?" I turned away. Then, after services, as we filled plates at the *oneg,* he squeezed my shoulder and said, "I guess I knocked it out of the park, Jackie boy. You think anybody could tell?" When I didn't answer, he snapped, "Oh for Chrissakes!"

"What a splendid thing to say in a synagogue," my mother hissed in his ear. She shook her head. "Whose Bar Mitzvah *is* this? Isn't it the *boy* you should be proud of?"

So we had one more mark against my father—my poor, gross father, who felt he wasn't worth very much, married to a woman who confirmed his opinion, father to a son who agreed. The more elegantly she acted, the louder and cruder he became. What would it have been like if he hadn't felt so ashamed, if he could have expressed his sweetness?

For there were times I saw his deeper nature—saw sweetness, tenderness, good humor, a dropping away of defenses. Sometimes he'd take me out after dinner for an ice cream soda—and he'd hold my hand, unashamedly, even when I was ten, eleven. Then there were times I'd take the subway down to visit him at the main office of Tires Incorporated, the firm owned by my uncle on 49th and 10th. My father would see me coming in, put his arm around my shoulder and pat, pat, pat. I felt the heat radiating from him. He'd show me around to the half-dozen muscular guys who changed customers' tires. I could see they liked him. He respected them, laughed with them. He was a different man.

But soon my uncle, Lloyd Clayton, came out of his inner office and called, "Is this what we pay you guys for?" And the tire changers went back to work. "You, too, Chuck, for Chrissakes," my uncle sang, his voice echoing through the high-ceilinged garage. My father shut down—still a smile on his face, now more a grin. He turned to me, "Say hello to your uncle. Tell him what you got on your report card."

"No time for that vain crap today, Chuck." Taking out his wallet, he handed me a crisp ten-dollar bill. "You take your pop out for lunch. I can't join you—I'm too busy working to pay your pop's salary."

"Thank your uncle," my father said. But when we left the office, he said, "It'd be better you don't tell your mother about the ten dollars. She'll get on her high horse and give me trouble."

***

So it was my uncle, the arrogant charmer, the bully, who was the special one in our family. Growing up poor in Chicago—his mother took in boarders—he studied shorthand and typing and became a court stenographer at fifteen, and then, during World War I, became secretary to a general who made him an officer straight out of civilian life. He taught himself to appear classy. In the twenties he made himself a success in the tire business and paid his siblings to change their names, when he changed his—from Louie Cohen to Lloyd Clayton. In a sense he became father of his family. When I knew him, he spent his evenings at the Stork Club. He owned almost a square block of West Side Manhattan. And he owned *us*. Owned my father, his older brother. He foisted on my father his worn-out, hand-me-down shoes. He owned even my mother, who made him so central—the center of our family story, affirming him, confirming his power through her envy and hatred. "The bully! The sonofabitch! Don't let him get his claws on you," she warned me, again and again.

He *was* a sonofabitch. He *was*. Sometimes my uncle took us out to the Sea Fare. He played the big shot. He'd tear a ten-dollar bill in half, hand one half to the waiter, an African-American, and say, "George [after the black conductors on the Pullman cars], you see this here ten-dollar bill? The other half is yours when you give us the service we know we can expect from you." Even at nine or ten, I was ashamed; I loathed my uncle. I wanted to walk out. I tried to catch the waiter's eye to say we weren't all like that. But the waiter just grinned—even, if I'm remembering correctly, chuckled.

***

These family stories, I keep telling them, as if they defined me, explained me. I hardly trust them anymore. I pretend they help me explain who I am. I should take them with a grain of salt.

Today, the Torah scroll, covered in velvet, with bells of silver crowning the spindles—while it's carried around the sanctuary to *be touched by the congregants,* the fat man catches my eye, looks away again. And, clearing his throat, not looking at me, says quietly, as if to legitimize his presence, "I'm here to say Kaddish for my son. It's his *yahrzeit*. The anniversary of his death."

"I'm so sorry."

We look at each other.

"Five years ago. A car crash. He was twenty-five."

"'May his memory be for a blessing.'"

"Thank you. He was a wonderful son. An accident. An icy road."

He sighs. I sigh. I don't tell him that I, too, lost an adult son. It's *his* time, the stranger's time, not mine. We nod at one another, we don't speak. I wish I could say something that matters. I feel for this mourning father as if I'd known him all my life.

The Torah service begins. Members of the congregation climb two steps to the bima to chant a blessing over the Torah scroll. Then the rabbi or another congregant reads a passage from the Torah. All over the world on this Saturday morning the same passage from Torah is being read. Glancing over, I see the stranger, the father, bent down, burrowed into his cupped hand, silently weeping.

I imagine touching his shoulder, imagine saying, *Listen – I'm going up to the bima next. Come with me. No one will mind. We'll take an* aliyah *together in honor of your son.* I don't make the offer – I don't want to embarrass him, don't want to embarrass myself.

So when it's time for my aliyah, I go up alone. From the bima I look out over the congregation – unusually full today. As I chant the blessing, I see faces meeting my face and faces turned inward. I wonder about their stories as I wonder about my own. How much do they hide? It's in the place where our stories dissolve that we are worthy.

Toward the end of the service, mourners stand to say Kaddish, an affirmation of holiness. The Kaddish is not in Hebrew but in Aramaic. I don't understand much of the Aramaic, but every time it's chanted or recited, I feel what the prayer is *doing*. In spite of the broken surface of our lives, in spite of our losses, our defenses, our self-deceptions, we praise. As if it's telling us we don't have to be complete—we can celebrate a completeness beyond ourselves. The praise changes us. It's a physical thing.

When the stranger stands, I stand up beside him, though this isn't an anniversary of the death of my son or of my parents. Does the stranger understand? My shoulder, my shirt sleeve, press the sleeve of his jacket. Again, I feel the heat emanating from him. We recite the Kaddish.

THREE

Good Blood

AROUND THE DINNER TABLE last night, I tried to tell a story. I was with family—my wife, my daughter, my son-in-law, my granddaughter and her boyfriend. I tell you about my audience to indicate how safe the situation was. More and more, as my Parkinson's has developed, when I begin to speak, especially in a group, my mind goes blank. My voice becomes rough and low. But even here, in the safety of family?

Well, maybe family doesn't feel so safe. My wife, my daughter, do turn to listen. My granddaughter, who has grown up on the other side of the country from us, doesn't particularly want to hear my story. Nor her boyfriend. I know that. And why should they? There was something on TV taking their attention. And I think there was a conversation going on. I was foolish to interrupt. But it's such a perfect story of healing, and I need a story of healing. All the parts fit together so well as to be not-quite-believable. Maybe it's more an urban legend than a true story full of odd parts that convey a depth, parts that stick out, that don't fit. Here everything fits too neatly. I don't quite believe this story, but I wanted to tell it. Someone at the table mentions Elton John; maybe his name reminds me of the story I want to tell.

A friend, no longer living, told it to me many years ago; he said he knew personally the generous Londoner, an executive, a gay man, who is at the center of the story. As I start to tell the story, I go blank, like a nervous child standing up in front of his class. My mouth begins to slur the words as if I'd drunk a little too much, and, trying to put the pieces into their proper relation, I struggle to get the words out. For a few seconds I forget who in the story has the blood sickness, and who gets the transplant. I can't even remember that it was bone marrow, not a kidney, not a transfusion. And by now I've lost my audience.

Why tell this story two decades old?

Now, next morning, alone, I remember the story perfectly—the Londoner, a vice-president of an international travel corporation, put himself on a list as a donor for a bone marrow transplant. Because he was gay, he'd been refused by the Red Cross as a blood donor, and this upset him very much. The registry for transplanting bone marrow tested him but didn't reject him. So why not sign on? He thought of it, I'm guessing here, as a moral kindness he'd likely never be asked to follow through on. It was so unlikely that he'd be a match. But then, only a few months later, he gets a call from the registry: he *is* a match.

A transatlantic match. A young man from—let's call

it Atlanta—with leukemia or myeloma—some cancer of the blood—desperately needs a transplant of bone marrow to stay alive. The registry tried a match in his family, then tried possible matches in the United States, but it's only he, the Londoner—let's call him James—who proves a perfect match. James doesn't give excuses and back down, though he knows it's not as easy as he first imagined: he has to be injected for five days before the procedure, a procedure lasting many hours; he knows it will keep him from work—and he's a busy man.

But he decides he'll go through with it.

The family of the sick young man flies him to England and puts James up in a private hospital. The next day his bone marrow will be drawn. But that evening, the young man's mother comes to the hospital room. And here is the first turn in the story. James, wanting to avoid an emotional scene, fears she's there to tell him how grateful she is—how grateful the family is. But instead, she asks him, "Is it possible that you might be Jewish? —that you might have Jewish blood?"

An absurd question. James wonders: Is this woman anti-Semitic? Is she afraid that her son's blood will be Jewish? James is struck dumb.

But no. The opposite. "You see," she says, "we're Jewish. Our family. I was hoping we could wait for a match with someone of Jewish blood."

James stares at her. Is she serious? He tells her, "That's up to your son. He's the one who'll live or die."

How do I know, how did my friend know, what she said, what he said? Of course, we don't. But I know that the sick young man decides, in spite of his mother, to go ahead with the transplant. Of course he does. Or else I'd be telling a different story—of a mother who was so rigid as to be willing to deprive her son of life. I wonder—no, it's not likely; perhaps the mother wasn't so severe, insisting on Jewish blood. Perhaps she was merely hoping that James was Jewish. But as I heard the story, she begged him not to go ahead with the procedure.

The next day bone marrow is drawn.

Skip ahead two or three years. The young man writes that he's healthy—he's in remission and has been remiss; he's bringing his wife and children to London—partly because he wants to thank James. James has saved his life.

A happy ending.

But James is a busy man and, according to my friend, a diffident, a reserved, man. The last thing he wants is to be flooded with expressions of gratitude. Besides, all this time the young man hasn't written. Now, James wonders, how can he avoid an emotional scene of hugs and tears? James pulls connections and buys the tickets for the American family—the young man, his wife, his two children—tickets that nobody can get for love or money for the Elton John concert at Wembley. Tickets and, I'll add—because it shows the effort James has made to avoid scenes of gratitude—a limo to take the Americans to Wembley. "I'm too busy to go with you, but I'm sure you'll have a lovely time."

All is well. But now comes a second turn in the story. Here enters Elton John.

On the phone the American is silent for a few seconds, and then says to James, "That's really kind of you. But to be frank, I've heard that Elton John is openly homosexual, and I can't subject my family to a homosexual performer."

James remembers the young man's mother. So here's the same family rigidity. James must think for a moment of taking a kind of sweet revenge. Who wouldn't? He must think of telling the American, "You're alive because of the blood of a gay man. It's inside you now, keeping you alive." Unless he were a saint, he must have thought of saying that. But James says nothing – says that he hopes the Americans have a good stay in London. "I can surely give away the Elton John tickets."

What generosity, not to take revenge.

A year or so later, my friend told me, James finds himself planning a business trip to Atlanta, and he writes the American asking him to make a contact. Why not? It turns out that the American is part of a wealthy and powerful clan. Communications cross the ocean back and forth. James is surprised, is embarrassed when the mayor's assistant comes to his hotel. At a ceremony in front of city hall, James is given the symbolic key to the city of Atlanta.

***

I especially don't trust this part of the story. I don't believe in the folk tale ending. But maybe I need it.

I wonder. Last night, why did I happen to think of this story to tell? Of course—it's a story about healing. The story came to me because of my own sickness, my struggle with Parkinson's. Nothing can replace the lost dopamine in my brain. Last night, I stumbled through my telling. I lost the plot points. My daughter and my wife, sitting with me at the table, did their best to listen to my broken pieces of story.

I'm grateful: this morning the words come easily. I remember the story, I can put the story together, pull myself together to write down this story of healing.

FOUR

Energy

I'D WRITE ABOUT my exhaustion from Parkinson's, but I'm too exhausted. Some joke. My chief symptom, doc, isn't the shakes. It's torpor. Sluggishness, lethargy, thickness in the head; what it feels like when you've got the flu.

"Are you sure it's Parkinson's?" a friend asks. "Your hands shake but not so much. Your face isn't all that frozen. You walk well."

"Thanks. Want me to shake for you a little? Should I maybe fall down?"

It exhausts me to defend my sickness—to name my symptoms as the effect of Parkinson's, to tell my friends what my neurologist has told me: the dopamine is slipping from my brain. "Just wait," I say. "Everything is sure to get worse, don't worry, give it time."

If I haven't got a little humor, what do I have?

Friends and family want to help, to cure me. If I listened to all the remedies they suggest, I'd be running from healer to healer. And who can run? They're being kind, I know. They want this ridiculous condition to end.

It discomfits them—disturbs them not to find closure. "Can't you *do* something? Have you thought of . . . ?" They name this panacea or that. They've heard about the value of dance, they've heard about fabulous results from boxing, from spin classes.

Explaining why I'm unwilling to try techniques my friends have heard about online, I find my exhaustion deepening. Abulia, lack of will, sits on me like a great sea creature. It's hard to breathe. When I'm asked to choose whether to do A or B, I say, "*You* choose. I don't care." You choose a movie, you choose a menu, you choose where we're going. This not-caring isn't simply a moral flaw. It's a symptom of Parkinson's—at least, of *my* Parkinson's. Once upon a time—say three or four years ago—I was plenty willful. Maybe too willful.

I take carbidopa levodopa, which tries to make up for the lost dopamine. It diminishes the shakes but doesn't touch my exhaustion. I take Ritalin, like an undergraduate with an exam coming up. It disguises exhaustion so I can work. I can write this. But soon I'm under water. I sleep, but waking from sleep I'm drowning, as if my cells were saturated. My head throbs. I hear faint voices, as from a low radio in another room; I know nobody's there. Sometimes the voices become a chorus far off, chanting in minor key, a fragment of a beautiful melody, over and over.

I want to find wholeness, as if my life had a pattern, as if the Parkinson's had a meaning, as if my childhood were relevant to my life now. I don't want my life now to be built on a mistake, like an auto accident. I want there to be design. Is there a design? I know there's at least an analogy: the frozenness of Parkinson's, the rigidity of living within a narrative that is also frozen. My mother. My father. My uncle Lloyd. All of us took parts in the same story. I can't seem to shed the story.

My exhaustion has a neurological source—the loss of dopamine in the brain. But it reminds me of my childhood sickness for which there was no apparent physical source: I was seven years old and got banged up in the playground, hurt a little when a wagon turned over on me—a pile-up of children. Maybe I was bruised—I can't remember. But after a few days, a new kind of pain began.

Not serious, the doctor said. Nothing wrong. Taking me to doctors became her occupation. She dressed up; we took a taxi. She took me to expensive doctors but never paid full price. "You should have arranged a reduction in fee with my secretary," one doctor challenged her. "But my dear," my mother said, "I needed to find the best doctor in New York, and I'm told you're the best. I knew you'd understand."

A follow-up fluoroscopy showed nothing. But the nagging discomfort in my stomach, which I now recognize as anxiety, kept on, kept on. We called it "butterflies in the stomach." I stayed out of school for months, most of second grade. I read, I played in my room, I sat in the kitchen with my mother. I sat with her when she was at her best.

And I believe I learned to focus on my own discomfort, on the butterflies. Learned the value of my discomfort. I've lived in pain—headaches, back aches—the way my mother lived in pain. The butterflies kept me home from school, where I had a teacher who, I was sure, despised me. I didn't lie about being unwell—I felt unwell. But when my mother asked me how I was this morning, the butterflies inside would become more active, and I'd stay home for another day, another week. Then another month. I'm wondering whether that became a template for using discomfort or pain later in my life. I learned to nurse my aches and pains, as recently, I've been nursing my exhaustion. I wasn't exactly malingering, but still somehow using my illness.

As my mother used hers. As she taught me to use mine—though she certainly didn't intend for me to focus on pain.

Mornings, my mother sat with me in the kitchen and told me stories. "God grant me long life as true as I'm standing here, I was in Flo Ziegfeld's apartment—some apartment, let me tell you—over the theater, and he said to me, 'Leah, you're something special. You know what's going on. Where did your family come from?'

"'From Russia, Mr. Ziegfeld,' I told him. 'I was born in Kishinev.' Well, the whole world knew Kishinev because of the terrible pogrom.

"'No!' he said. I said, 'Yes, Mr. Ziegfeld. From Russia. I came to America when I was five.' 'My God,' he said, 'and you are every bit an American girl.'"

This was like getting a PhD in American Girliana.

Performing for me in the kitchen, she lifted the hem of her old, stained, blue housedress, placed a quarter between her calves, a quarter between her knees. "Flo Ziegfeld told me that he has his chorus girls do this to see if their legs are perfect. But of course, would your mother ever be a chorus girl?" She loved to tell me stories of her life—true or exaggerated. Gay nights in Paris . . . a wealthy broker who wanted to marry her. She told me stories and took down my own stories on her Underwood. She was my first writing teacher. I strode back and forth telling her a story, a poem, an idea. I was a little Napoleon. My mother, hitting the keys with force, made my ideas real.

Why, then, would I want to return to school? After a few months I did return—to a new class. And gradually the discomfort in my stomach disappeared.

It's no accident that for most of this time, my father was in California taking care of his father. My uncle ordered him to go, paid his salary when he was out there. My mother was sad and bitter. She didn't know what to do with her life. I wasn't big enough to fill it.

Here's a letter I found from her to my father. Did he bring it back with him from California? I quote verbatim:

Dearest Chuck,

Your Thursday letter came today. With the snapshots. Your face looks good, and you don't look too heavy. But your pants need pressing, and don't they wear ties in California?

Please, Chuck, don't say to me, "please be sweet." I have been sweet too long. It is now into the sixth month since you went away. That's nice, isn't it? I don't say you went there out of choice, but after all, you are not a dummy, and if you are a human being, you could have said the second month you were there, "I am going home to my wife and child."

Well, you are as you are, and I will never change you, Chuck.

Enclosed you will find a short letter from Jackie. Why he loves you is more than I can say. He is deserving of a devoted father not a dummy who is shoved around by his brother.

I will have to pay Hoover $14.65 for repair Thursday. Remember, Chuck, I have been a good wife, and a girl a man doesn't have to be ashamed of. And I have given you all my love, Chuck dear. But your staying away has disgusted me beyond repair.

Love, Leah

Hearing her voice in that letter, I feel so strongly my mother's presence. I see her lying across the bed afternoons when I was home from school or came home from school. Every afternoon, even when my father returned from California, she became exhausted. All that charm of the morning was gone. My mother didn't have Parkinson's, but my own exhaustion from Parkinson's helps me understand what she was going through. What she was going through helps me understand my Parkinson's.

She didn't sleep well at night. She slept, she woke. She'd smoke, crush out her cigarette in an ash tray and smoke again. I'd wake to find her standing guard in the doorway to my bedroom, cigarette between her fingers. Mornings were her sweet time. Much of the afternoon, she slept. I wasn't sympathetic. I was confused, angry, at her virtual absence. I wandered the dead apartment or walked across Central Park to the Metropolitan Museum.

I didn't understand how depressed she really was. Napping, waking in the afternoon, not rested, bitter, she could hardly speak to me. She made dinner for me, and when my father was with us in New York, for my father and me. But she herself ate cottage cheese and sour cream with raw vegetables. Her fingers became smeared. Staggering back to bed, she smudged the walls. I don't think she drank—certainly not enough to make her stagger. At six, my father came home and—furious—he washed the spots on the walls, and he cried in his beautiful high tenor, "I work all day and look what she does to me!" Then she got up, old crone, stumbling, cursing him in Yiddish or in an English that had the feeling of Yiddish—of her home language: My blood is black, black is my blood . . . her fingernails, like claws, reaching for him.

I waited for the nightly fight to begin. The waiting was worse than the fight. "You're bringing the kid up to be a bum. Want him to think money grows on trees? You, you're bleeding me!"

"Come on, big boy, you want to fight?" She put up her fists.

At her better times, she sat at the kitchen table with us, smoking, while we ate and my father complained. At bad times she dug her nails into the flesh of her own upper arm leaving bloody tracks. Or she went to the kitchen drawer for a suicide knife—as gesture—*you see what you've driven me to?* – or stuck her head in the gas oven—as gesture. Some gesture! He yelled louder. Now, as if her defenses had collapsed—all the charm, all the contempt—she feigned fainting, as if stunned, a cow at the slaughterhouse hit with a hammer. Her eyes were blank and rolling. Gaga. Her mouth hung open.

He pushed her away, she crumpled to the floor. It was both real and theater.

When she collapsed, he became uneasy. "Get up, goddammit, Leah!" He half-carried, half dragged her back to bed to get rid of her. "What kind of a life she gives me? What kind of life?"

Sometimes she wept. We could hear her through the closed bedroom door.

Sometimes he went to her and comforted.

Now I know what she must have been going through. In the World to Come, I'll tell her I understand. I know, I know.

I imagine energy flowing through a human body—like a mist, but even more invisible. Not substance but electrical charges feeding the cells. Energy seeps out and away. The cells are starving, shrinking. I lay down to rest, but rest doesn't restore me.

It's the mist, its energy that makes us up. The cells—bones and brain—are only the structure, like a software platform, like frame construction before a house is sheathed, before the walls are hammered into place. The frame isn't the house, though without the frame there wouldn't be a house.

Energy isn't lost. It's real and unending. When we die, structure disintegrates, disappears, not the energy. Energy flows away to fill new structures, to make itself into new structures. But to say "flows" makes energy sound like substance, and that's wrong. Dylan Thomas writes, *And death shall have no dominion*. Is this way of seeing illusory, merely comforting? Or is it simply true, not fantasy at all?

This is what it feels like: the energy that composes me, that creates me, is dissipating, disappearing. Sickness has simply sped up the process we all go through. Don't be afraid, I tell myself.

I remember my mother in the hospital, so sweet, all the bitterness gone, saying, near the very end, *don't worry. I'm not afraid of dying.*

Was she really unafraid or was that more of my mother's theatrics? Now, she whispered, "How are we going to make coffee for all the nurses?"

"Do you know where you are, Mom?"

"Naturally. In the hospital. You think I'm a fool? They explained it to me, I have an aneurism. It's called an aneurism. But when we go downstairs to the apartment, someone has to feed the nurses. It's only right." So she tried to pull out her IV, discard her nasal cannula. I pressed her shoulders down and tried to distract her. We were in the middle of an Isaac Bashevis Singer story. I picked up from where we left off, though the story didn't matter—it was the music of the stories she needed. She settled, she beckoned me to her with a forefinger. "I'm going to sleep for a while. You can make the coffee for the girls. You know how. Haven't I taught you?"

"You taught me. I remember."

"Your poor father never learned to make a decent cup of coffee. Maybe you can teach him."

"Teach Dad? Do you remember what happened to Dad?"

"He's dead, of course, don't you think I know that? I was there, wasn't I? He fell down in the living room, he fell like a tree. My Chuck, my Charlie, my husband, my wonderful husband."

My father had died three years before. My mother rewrote the story of their marriage. It became a beautiful marriage. "You never understood him," she told me some months before. "And he never understood you."

"Well," she said the day she died, "and wasn't he wonderful? I'm not saying he was perfect, your father, but he loved me very much. Sometimes, for very good people, death comes like that. The Divine kiss, they call it. He asked me what I was making for dinner, and he fell down. Fell like a tree. He was gone before he touched the floor."

"I know, Mom."

"Now I need to sleep. Later you can read to me again."

Five

How to Heal Parkinson's

LADIES 'N GENTS don't tell a soul, but fact is, you can't do a hell of a lot about healing Parkinson's. We, bourgeois in the Flaubertian sense, we're so used to making demands on reality when something isn't going right, that we don't take no for an answer. Saul Bellow writes somewhere that being bourgeois means figuring out, as you slip and fall on a neighbor's icy sidewalk, the insurance money you'll win. But Parkinson's is not like a twisted ankle or a broken window or a leaky pipe. No, indeed, ladies and gents, it's not. *"I'm going to fight this; I'm going to fix this."* A joke.

We speak of illness through the metaphor of war: *the battle against cancer*. "So sorry you have a health challenge," a friend wrote.

Some challenge! Like unarmed slaves "challenging" wild beasts in the arena.

The trap is, the joke is, that while it's foolish to think you're going to beat a sickness like Parkinson's, you're just not going to give up trying.

So I spend my money on micronutrients and a treadmill. I remember to stand straight and practice my balance. Mornings, I pray. Doctors don't know everything. I nap. Waking, I hear the voices from another room—those friendly baritone voices in my head. I pretend to imagine they're discussing my case.

What, then, I imagine them asking, is to be done?

Waking, especially from my nap in the afternoon, I'm aware of my whole body trembling. Opening my eyes, I see black dots hovering in the middle of the air. I'm more exhausted getting up than when I lay down—I could fall right back to sleep. But then how will I sleep tonight?

What can I do to give me back my energy? Am I worse than I was yesterday? Which pills should I take? I monitor my exhaustion, though I know what a mistake this is. "Monitor" is cognate with "admonish." "Admonition." A warning. But why warn when you can't change anything?

What's to be done? What's best is *not to do.* Do, and you're undone, symptoms intensified.

I learned as a child to exhibit my pains and illnesses to my mother. Learned from my mother to monitor, to groan and sigh. As a child I developed stomach aches, headaches. I brought them to her. I learned to pay attention to my pain. I wanted her attention, too, and then became angry when she gave it.

As I'm remembering our talk, I must have been eight or nine years old. But we always talked like this.

"Why," my mother said, "should a boy like you have a

headache? *My* son? Why should *my son* have a headache?" She tried out remedies on me and she asked, did this help? Did that help? Until I said I was feeling better, she didn't stop. I wanted her to stop; I didn't want her to stop.

She suffered and taught me to express my suffering; she drank boiled water without tea to ease the gas in her stomach. The heartburn. She gave herself enemas. She sighed. "As God is my witness . . . you should never know how your mother suffers."

"Stop, stop! I do know. You never stop telling me."

"Don't worry. I'll stop soon enough. You want me to stop? Should I stop for good?"

I shook my head, parodying the way she shook her head. She shut her eyes.

If I asked, "What's the matter, Mom? What's hurting?" She'd sigh: "The matter? Why, nothing is the matter. Isn't that what you think? Everything is sweet. My life is so sweet."

But if I *didn't* ask, she'd say, "You're all I've got in this world? Don't you know that? And you don't ask how your mother is? Don't you want to know?"

"Of course I want to know."

"You think your mother is a complainer."

I laughed. "Well, don't you complain a lot?"

She ignored this. "I've got a swell marriage. Simply swell. My husband goes out to California for months and months to take care of his father. Who wouldn't complain?"

"You're right. But he's back now. Grandpa's dead."

"You think he's such a pleasure when he's home? Let me tell you a secret. This is between us. Your father means well, but perhaps—just perhaps—he married the wrong woman. As perhaps—just perhaps—I married the wrong man. I should have stayed in the business. That's the truth. In fashion, the fashion industry. In *haut couture*. If I called Old Man Bonwit on the phone this morning, he'd ask me to come back and work for him."

"Well, why don't you?"

"You don't think so. You think I couldn't?"

"I didn't mean that. Mom? Why *don't* you?"

"The fashions have passed me by a long time ago, my darling." She sighed and nodded, nodded and sighed. "And am I strong enough to take a position? You know what that entails? Besides, don't I have to take care of you and your father?"

What would it mean—to stop trying to fix myself? To let go and simply live? Why is it so seductive to monitor my symptoms when I know it doesn't help? Would it be like giving up my mother? So? Isn't it time, for godsakes? Don't I, at least, need to give up my mother's strategy?

But that's wrong; it wasn't really a strategy. She wasn't trying to end her suffering. She needed to feel it. Or else she would have gone crazy. She needed *me* to feel it.

When, twenty-five years ago, I began to light candles on Friday nights, I remembered my mother turning to the shelf in our kitchen where she lit candles, turning and murmuring something in Yiddish. But they weren't Shabbat candles she lit; they were memorial glasses. The glasses would burn all night, all day. We'd use the empties as drinking glasses. My mother grew up in an Orthodox household. How could she not know the difference? And if they really were yahrzeit lights, 24-hour memorial candles, who was she mourning and why only on Friday nights? Was it just a mistake?

She held her hand over her eyes and wept—though on Shabbat we are supposed to be joyous. She was solemn as she nodded at the candles. She never explained. Now I think I understand: she was mourning her lost Jewish family, her sweet childhood, and her lost hopes—mourning her stifled self that once held such promise. Shabbat was the time for her to face irretrievable loss.

If my father came into the kitchen and saw her lighting the candles, he'd slap the air, quick, back and forth, as if to expunge a stench, and say, "What a load of old-fashioned crap." He was irritated. He was counting the cost of the candles. My mother would turn to me and say, "You hear that? A real Jewish gentleman. What a charming, cultivated man I married."

"And you," he snapped. "Ain't you some charming woman in that dirty housedress of yours."

But the truth is, she *was* a charming woman. She had her ways.

I remember this: I must have been nine or ten. We're sitting near the back on a Madison Avenue bus, coming home from shopping or from the doctor's. She points up at an office building. Right away I know what's coming, and it's embarrassing as hell. I look away.

"Lookh, *mein* Benny," she calls out in thick pretend Yiddishe accent, "Lookh at all de big buildinks!"

"Shh, Mom! Please."

"Vatz de matta? You's so ashamed by your immigrant modder, de vay she talks?"

Passengers give me dirty looks—or I imagine they do. *Your poor mother!* Is it possible they don't know she's kidding? It's possible. This is during the war—say 1944. New Yorkers are used to refugees. Me, I can hear the put-on—it's so obvious. But my mother's first language was Yiddish; her accent can be as authentic as she wants to make it.

"So, Benny, mein boy, you don't want be seen vit your immigrant modder who loves you?"

"She's kidding," I say loudly to a listening public. "My name isn't Benny. She's kidding. We're Americans."

No one's looking our way. It's time to change for a crosstown bus. My mother says to everyone, in upper-class British accent with clear articulation, "Lovely weather we're having. Don't you agree, Benjamin?"

Look! I can turn myself into an immigrant or a privileged, educated American. Just like that I can invent myself and reinvent myself. And you, my son, can be my audience.

Or this later memory, from when I must have been twelve or thirteen:

Say it's a morning when I didn't have school, and she decided to take me shopping downtown. She'd dress up in her Persian wool coat and Persian wool hat, a blue silk scarf at her throat, and she became my elegant, witty mother.

We get into the crowded elevator at Sak's Fifth Avenue—the metal inner gate, the outer doors, shut. One glance and I can see in her face what's coming—I knew her routine of tantalizing the folks in the elevator. She stage-whispers, "So. So, there she was, half naked!" *Naked* I didn't expect. I'm embarrassed. But also amused.

Looking around the crowded elevator to make sure no one's overhearing, knowing *everyone's* overhearing, she says, as if continuing to tell me a story, ". . . So, my dear, you *know* about his luxurious apartment, the duplex at the Beresford. Remember, I took you there? And you've heard what a powerful man he is. *And* of course you know Isabel. Well, according to Isabel, he told her in his big voice, 'Time to take off your clothes.' And, he told her, she'd better listen. Well, she stands at the top of the stairs and begins to take off her fabulous clothes. She's no prude, that Isabel."

My mother swivels around to make sure no one's listening. Ha ha. Everyone's looking anywhere but at her. "But you can imagine, my boy, *how* she takes off her clothes. Slowly, half tantalizing him, half holding back, hoping that Charlie gets there."

By now we're on the second floor, doors open, doors close. "What happened, Mom?" I ask, collecting myself.

"Did Charlie get there?" Now we pass three, we're up to four. "The doorbell rings. It's Charlie." We're up to six. Men's clothing, the elevator half full. My mother's comic timing: As the elevator slows and just as the door opens, she says, "Now he takes out a pistol from an end table and points it . . ." And we walk out of the elevator, while the customers, looking at the elevator ceiling, strain to hear. The elevator door closes, and no one finds out who the powerful rich man is, whom he points his gun at, or whether Isabel finally gets naked. I relax, I let go a laugh.

Now, seventy years later, I know who the powerful man of her fantasy is. Not just my uncle, whom she hated with murderous hatred and obsessed over with envy, but the original dream figure—magical avatar of wealth and power and American success: shape of the longing of the immigrant girl.

She couldn't stand it—not being the great success, the brilliant lady upon whom the lights of New York shone. She thought she'd married a man of wealth and power who could give her the life she demanded. She was so deeply dissatisfied. She lived in the story of the gap between how she wanted to live and how she was actually living.

I could say that her rage, unassimilated, exhausted her. But perhaps exhaustion was her unconscious strategy; she learned to fall into exhaustion and pain as a way of handling, quieting, her rage.

She taught me to monitor myself.

Then what's to do? Can I unlearn? Can I suffer my exhaustion without monitoring it? Can I be like the three-legged dog that makes do—who doesn't whine, doesn't focus on the missing limb?

The last few years of her life, while my father became weaker and she sported a cane, my mother's rage quieted, her exhaustion diminished. They became a peaceful couple. When my wife and I visited, there was no shouting, no shutting and opening windows so the neighbors wouldn't hear—or *would hear.* She spoke sweetly to him. "Chuck, dear, would you like a nice sandwich?" He didn't complain; she didn't complain. I couldn't understand. Somehow, she no longer had to feel her terrible dissatisfaction. She was content. The fighting was over.

Then she became a peaceful widow, and she lived another story entirely. "Poor fool," That's how she remembered him. But the words were said with tenderness. And when I reminded her that there had been hard times in our life together, she'd say, "What do you mean 'hard'? I've been a happy wife and mother. Yes, there were quarrels, but what married couple doesn't have their quarrels?"

After my father died, my Uncle Lloyd changed; he became a responsible brother-in-law; he moved my mother into a pretty little apartment on Central Park West, and he paid the rent. Once a week he'd send his chauffeur to take my mother shopping. "It's wonderful that Lloyd takes care of you," I said.

"Well—and don't I deserve it?" She smiled. "But I must say, I must say, he's been a little bit of all right." Then she added, "Well—and shouldn't he be? Your father was as good as gold to him. He was so loyal—such a loyal brother." She added, "Besides . . . Lloyd knows the kind of woman I am."

The fighting was over, and with it the self-torture. It was over not because she was defeated. She had declared a truce. No—better than a truce: she pretended to herself that there was no struggle, that there never had been a struggle. She was simply the gracious lady she'd always imagined herself.

What is to be done? Of course. A lesson from my mother: stop fighting the loss. Change the story. Can I eliminate the exhaustion? No. Can I treat it as simply the way things are? Just as I can't, no matter how hard I try, run a marathon or play in the NFL, can I accept this incapacity? Will it help if I refuse to accept? What's to do? Maybe no more than tell myself that this exhaustion and all the other joys of Parkinson's, they're simply who I am now. Would that be lying?

SIX

The Angry Bear

I WAKE IN THE MORNING ragged, barely able to get myself out of bed. I hear an alarm and wake myself to turn it off before it wakes Sharon. But there's been no alarm except in my sleep. Tricked again. Pain hovers at the edges of dream. Still in bed, half awake, I monitor my aching body, my aching head, though I know it's better not to monitor. My body says, *Parkinson's*. I slip out of bed so as not to wake Sharon. Trembling fades.

Once I begin to exercise, I'm not so broken. I can meditate and pray morning prayers. But prayer is much harder than before Parkinson's. Why is it so hard? I've chanted morning prayers for the past twenty-five years. Haven't they deepened me so that when I need prayer, I have it? This focus on my own condition is the opposite of prayer. Self, self! I want to be God-centered; thankful for my wife, for my children, for all the work I've done in my life, writing, and teaching. Isn't God in my heart especially in pain and age?

I remember my father as an old man. In his last few years, he was on Elavil for depression. Not the same condition, but like mine, my Parkinson's, something that can take over your life. Growing up, I knew my father as a big, burly man, not smart, often angry, an angry bear. But when I was an adult, visiting my parents every few months with my first wife and our daughter, I saw him fade, more and more absorbed by depression, growing more and more out of it as if in time-lapse photography. How shrunken his face became, how much weight he lost, so that the bones of his shoulders, once padded with muscle and too much flesh, stuck out. How gentle he became.

He kissed us, the three of us. "How's my boy? You're all right in my book." His face felt cool where once it was hot and tinged with sweat. Then, instead of sitting with us in the living room, he stood, rocking slightly, near the bathroom door, waiting for a sign from his body that he would be able to defecate.

When I was a child, though I longed to be his friend, he was my enemy. I couldn't imagine him as weak. But as he grew old, he became very weak, and I didn't need to defend myself against loving him. Taking me aside, my mother murmured, "You see? You see what he's like?" Turning to my father, she said, in the most loving voice, "Chuck, maybe, dear, you'd like some tea?"

He shook his head. "I gotta go to the bathroom."

"You can go to the bathroom later. Don't you want

to see your son and his family? Weren't you telling me all morning that you want to see them?"

I put my arm around his bony shoulder.

***

Now I'm old; I wake exhausted. Hard work to get out of bed, put my feet on the floor. Then I sit, as if I were doped up on a narcotic. I sit dumbly, blank, then struggle to my feet, dress, go into the other room and begin my exercises.

I'm older than my father was when he died. He's very present to me. More than present. It's as if he were inside me or I were inside him.

A year before his death I was called by my mother: "Your father is in the hospital. At Mt Sinai. The doctors, my dear, want to give him shock therapy for his depression. They want you to sign off on it."

"Why me? Why me?"

"So many questions. You can do me a favor and come to New York? Is that too much to ask?" Then, exasperated, she said, "Or *don't* come."

In those days shock therapy was crude. To take responsibility for ordering it felt terrible, to have this power over him unbearable. I was alone—my first wife and I were separated. I took the shuttle from Boston. My father was sitting up in a hospital bed, speaking to himself as if in another language. They must have put him on a heavy psychotropic like Thorazine.

For some reason I didn't have to sign the release. It

was my mother, after all, who signed, and then the doctors decided not to jolt him with shock, maybe afraid of his heart giving out.

Why was I so moved?

I flew home that night—I needed to teach the next day. A woman I was seeing, lover and political comrade, met me at the plane. I wept, I wept, and I needed her comfort. Embarrassed for me, always a cool customer, she stiffened at my embrace. I knew our romance was going to be short-lived.

It was a year later that my father died. Again and again I hear my mother on the phone: "He fell like a tree felled in the forest. Your Uncle Lloyd is taking care of all the arrangements. Do you think you might come to your father's funeral?" As if to say, *what kind of son are you? I don't expect very much from you.*

"You know I'll come, of course I'll come. Dad and I, we made up a long time ago. And even if we hadn't . . . I'll be there in a few hours, stay with you tonight."

I took the shuttle from Boston. We didn't sit Shiva, didn't know enough to sit Shiva. Why didn't we know? Why didn't my mother know? Hadn't she grown up in an Orthodox household? We sat with my Aunt Ann in the kitchen and told each other stories. My mother wanted me to know how good he was, how close they were to one another—already rewriting the story of their life together. In fact, she'd started rewriting it a few years before, when he'd quieted down and had become soft as an angel.

My father's funeral was at Riverside Memorial Chapel on Amsterdam and 76th; after, I drove with my Uncle Lloyd behind the hearse to the cemetery in Queens. No one said prayers. That's how I remember it. We merely looked at the spot of ground in which my father was to be buried. It wasn't until 1992 that I came to Judaism, said prayers every day, attended services. It was up to me to recite the Kaddish, but when my father died, I didn't know what the Kaddish was. That night and the next day and the next I called up women I knew in the city. I visited them. I went from the West Village to the upper West Side to the lower East Side. I cried, the women comforted. I stayed over with one, then with another. Everyone dies, but a surviving son may become, for a while, special, and may be eligible for a reward for suffering. My grief was real, but I was flooded with sexual desire. I was ashamed of myself but couldn't stop.

***

Now, half a century later, my condition brings me close to him. He's inside my skin. I look out through his eyes. Strange. He was so different from me when I was a child and felt like his victim. He was happy at work—I've said this—well liked among the tire changers and salesmen at work. But so crude; rough, angry at home, especially about spending money. He shouted. *You're both bleeding me to death!*

At times he tried to get close to me—or to the "real" boy he wished me to be. Once he took me to watch boxing at St. Nicholas Arena on Columbus. He took me partly as a statement to my mother. He wasn't going to let me remain a goddamn "mama's boy." We had seats close to the ring where we could hear the thud of blows and see, even feel, the sweat spray off the bodies of the fighters. The place stank of sweat. But it was the blood and the shouting that really got to me, and my father's gruff "Hit the sonofabitch!"

My father had boxed Golden Gloves as a teenager. Out of condition, he weighed two hundred pounds, not all of it muscle, but when he'd thump fist into palm and bellow, "Use your right hand, you shmuck!" he seemed like some dangerous beast. He was in his element. He hit fist into palm. Everyone was yelling. And the blood—I was scared but was handling it until one of the fighters split open the other guy's cheek under an eye and blood sprayed out with the sweat. Drops of blood spattered my shirt!

"Christ, we'll never get the blood off," my father wiped with his handkerchief, cursing the cost of a shirt. At that, I got sick over my shirt, over my pants.

"Aaah, you sissy!" My father took out a handkerchief, rubbed away the puke, tossed the handkerchief under the seat. "A little blood for chrissakes. Whadaya think this was—a merry-go-round? Now I'll never hear the end of it from your mother."

And then there were the car rides. If someone cut Dad off or honked him, he took it as a personal insult. At the red light he'd jump out of the car and pound on the window of the driver who'd given him offence. "You got something to say to me? Why don't you get out of that car, mister?" No one ever took him up on it. The theater of it made me laugh. If my mother was with us, she'd shake her head. "Some gentleman I married! Chuck, please just let me out of the car. I'll take a taxi home."

***

But then there were times during my childhood when my father grew soft. He'd ask me to walk with him up to 86th Street for ice cream. On the way, he took my hand in his big, meaty hand. It was his way of apologizing for yelling. "I don't mean to be a bad guy."

"Me, too. I'm sorry, too."

"I ever tell you this? When you were born," my father said, "your grandfather—my Dad—gave me, as a gift for a baby, a belt to use on you—the way he used to whop me. He meant well. That was the old days. All I had to do was look at him the wrong way."

"And you never used that belt on me."

"Right. That's right. Hey, listen. You're okay in my book."

A friend of mine once told me that he didn't begin to have a relationship with his father until his father died. I feel the same. Aging and Parkinson's and the long process of mourning have given me the beginning of an understanding.

SEVEN

Fantasies of Disaster

I'D THOUGHT THAT, once diagnosed, Parkinson's worsened geometrically, asymptotically, till the sufferer would be unable to move, till the body froze absolutely and he entered a state in which nothing moves, nothing at all. When I drool or find it hard to swallow or when my hands shake or body trembles or my sense of smell seems to have disappeared, I interpret the problem as a sign of the future, a predictor of paralysis. When the words don't come out of my mouth and my brain seems to go blank, I grow afraid. Is this going to get worse and worse? And what about my vivid dreams and auditory hallucinations—the voices? It's ominous.

I do my exercises; I wonder if they help.

Maybe they do help. Anyway, I find I haven't gotten increasingly disabled. Maybe I'm using the wrong time-scale—should be imagining, in fantasies of disaster, the next decade, not the next month or year. For I have good days and bad days, morning exhaustion and afternoon clarity. I wake in the night and, yes, stumble a little, shaky, on my way to the bathroom, lean slightly to one side—left shoulder high, right shoulder low, fall from foot to foot. But I catch myself, stay more or less in balance.

I've spoken to Parkinson's patients who dance or play tennis. It doesn't have to be the end of life. In a way, Parkinson's is a gift, forcing me, enticing me, to change my life. Not that I wouldn't prefer to decline such a gift. Thanks, but no thanks.

I'm not to be given the choice. Here are my choices: to liberate the life within my life or to curl up and die. Or, accept my condition and find the blessings within it, or struggle against it and curse my luck.

Let me find the blessings. Let me pray.

***

It's hard for me, knocked out as I am from Parkinson's, to recite morning prayers. I wonder, what's the point? What's going to happen if I pray? Am I praying for help? What kind of help? Will God grant healing—enter my body and heal me? Am I praying in advance in gratitude?

What am I supposed to be grateful for? For not being crushed, as yet, by the full load—with the staggering, the frozen stumbling I've seen in those who've had Parkinson's for decades—seen their clumsy, timid walk behind an aluminum walker?

Shouldn't I feel blessed that I can speak, can still walk with long strides? I should, I should. And I am blessed, surely, in my wife, in my children and their mates, in friends. We're blessed with a beautiful, safe place in which to live, enough resources not to worry where the next meal is coming from.

So I begin: *Modeh ani – I give thanks before You* – and I chant some of the prayers that follow. But how exhausted I am, half asleep, really, so that prayers seem a duty, gratitude mere words. That's shameful. What can I offer honestly? *Dear God, I pray to be given the strength to pray.*

> *Heal us, Lord and we shall be healed*
> *Deliver us and we shall be delivered*
> *For You are our song of praise.*

But then, what happens as Parkinson's creeps up on me, what if I don't heal? For who, after all, heals from Parkinson's? *If You heal us, we shall be healed.* Here's a different possibility: Suppose healing is always delivered the moment we pray, but we, we don't know it, because we're looking for the wrong kind of healing.

Do not turn us away empty-handed.

Suppose we've been blessed and don't know it. Like picking up a winning ticket from the floor but mistaking it for a tossed-away scrap of paper. *You hear the prayers of Your people.*

A complete recovery from heaven. Refuah sheleima min hashamayim.

Am I playing with words? Yesterday I saw a sufferer with Parkinson's stumbling behind his wife. Inching along, literally by inches, a step, a step, a foot in four or five seconds. Will that be me in a few years? Can I become that crippled and still praise God for healing me? Only if I step beyond myself.

What does it mean to speak of healing? Simply to ask the question, to struggle with the question, is to step beyond the curing of disease or undoing of incapacity. Suppose the self that prays simply for healing of flesh finds something different, more important: an opportunity for deepening. A wholeness. May it be so with me. *Open my lips and my mouth will declare your praise.*

> *Cause us to return, our Father, to Your Torah. Bring us back to You.*

To Your *Torah*—which means Your Truth. Return? As if we'd been there at some earlier time. And when was that? When have I ever lived by Your Truth? What does it mean: *to return?* Haven't I always been separate from You? Long before I was diagnosed with Parkinson's, I belonged to that fragment I called my *self*. The prayer imagines wholeness, a life that may be lived in harmony with You. But haven't I often been false, though I longed for a true life? I've lived in my family story, not in the world.

I've always been a master at speaking truth while being false in the process. In my prayers at home or in synagogue I rattle off the Hebrew though I don't understand half the words I'm chanting. In a political group or a reading group or a group of friends, I know the esthetic and ideological markers that will impress. I speak to impress.

Not only impress others—I speak to impress myself. To feel strong.

Not *speak*. *Spoke* is more accurate. For now, with the flowering of Parkinson's, I speak very little in a group, since it's likely I'll be tongue-tied if I try. But I remember what it was like to say true things, valuable things, but say them in order to shine.

Sometimes I think that the symptoms of Parkinson's express a purging. As if the poor body, poor brain, were sick of falsity. I may not replace lost dopamine, but maybe I can get in touch with my wholeness, with Your Truth.

What is my wholeness, what is my truth?

You are the resurrector of the dead.

The prophet Ezekiel, in the Writings, participates in a miracle of resurrection. But as I read the beautiful passage, the miracle is not that God plucks bones from the ground. Ezekiel is asked by God, "Can these bones live?" And they do live. But I wonder: isn't God making metaphor, making dream-truth rather than magic? "I open your graves and cause you to come up out of your graves as My people . . ." We are meant to awaken, to hear the Word of the Lord. That's the real resurrection. From the falsity of selfhood to full life.

In the seventeenth century, *Vanitas,* a sub-genre of Dutch and Flemish painting, might show a table top of flowers . . . and skulls grouped like fruit in a bowl. Perhaps a young woman flirts with herself in a mirror, while scattered over a table, or revealed on the back of the mirror: skulls, skulls, often piles of skulls —sculpturally patterned: a design of death. Can these bones live?

Memento mori.

***

For Your deliverance we hope all day. Before I die, I want to live a true life.

Parkinson's won't kill me. But it's a preparation for death. A rehearsal. For I know I'll lose more and more of myself, more and more. Everyone I know has some malady. The difference is that most hope for a cure. Because I don't, as the old life disintegrates, I may be forced to treat my sickness as opportunity for new life. I pray: Don't turn away from me. Teach me, in the time I have left, to live closer to Your Truth.

Look upon our affliction. And redeem us speedily.

Look upon us, see what you've made, see what we've done with what was given. Perhaps all You do, Dear One, is look upon our affliction—our lives Your work of art. But that's not enough. We're the dancers, I say again, You, both dreamer and audience. Enter into the dance. Touch us, dance with us. Become part of our dance. Lead us to redemption.

EIGHT

Radical Hero

HERE'S A PHOTOGRAPH of me that one of my students took some time between spring, 1967 and spring, 1969. In this black and white photo, I'm standing on a wooden pie crate on Commonwealth Avenue at Boston University; I seem to be caught in the middle of making a speech. I gotta say, I look terrific—passionate, forceful. So young, it seems to me now. *So* young. Some other guy. I'm holding up a mimeographed sheaf of handouts, fomenting against the war in Vietnam and maybe attacking the complicity of the university with the war. From the lower left of the photo, a young woman, smiling, looks up at me.

I look happy, not angry. Yet I remember how angry I was in those days—and for good reason. I spoke at teach-ins, wrote articles, felt the seriousness of our fight against the war, against the draft, against racism and American imperialism. Almost every night I was at a meeting. Some weekends I protested in Boston or New York and once got jailed protesting in D.C.

Why then am I grinning in this photograph? Maybe I'm being heckled and I'm laughing with the heckler. Maybe I'm enjoying my role as public speaker—maybe enjoying it too much: conscious of my falsity, I'm laughing at myself. When I look back at that street photo, I see a comfortable, strong leader—and I know how false that is.

***

I've never been a leader; I always felt like a fraud in the role. In prep school—a day school off Central Park West—I was an outsider, a scholarship boy, bullied most days, especially by a two-hundred-pound fool I'll call Arnold. He'd wait on the stairs for me and grin and ask, each day the same, "Aren't you gonna shake my hand? And here I thought you were my friend." If I didn't shake, he'd grab my arm and twist it behind my back until I howled. If I shook his hand, he might just grin and let me go. Sometimes, he did. Hopeful, I'd shake his hand; usually he'd squeeze, squeeze until I howled. If I howled, he'd squeeze harder, punch me hard in the gut or the arm. He was no fighter—but he was big and strong and mean.

I wasn't really hurt; my hand was sore day after day. But worse, I was fearful and humiliated. The self I took away from those torture sessions was weak, ashamed. I'd have gone to the principal, but the principal was a lush who commanded no authority—he couldn't run a school. Finally, I paid for protection—by doing homework for a powerful guy; let's call him Steve, an athlete, a strong leader. The athlete—Steve was quarterback of the school team, as I remember—had his own reasons for defending me—not just making a deal for homework.

Steve despised Arnold—because Arnold bragged about his family's wealth and about the chauffeur who drove him to school, picked him up after school, partly because Arnold pretended he was a big shot when it was obvious he was weak—he had expensive clothes but no friends—and was as much an outsider as I was with my hand-me-down clothes and my scholarship. Next day, when Arnold asked to shake, Steve, who had been waiting on the landing above for the opportunity, came storming, from the landing above, down the staircase at him, slammed him against the wall, shoved him down the stairs, and went at him—smacked him in his fat gut again and again.

I was safer after that. But I'd developed a shamed self. An outsider self, relying on outside help. I denied I was faking. To be a radical—isn't that always to be outside? But at some level I knew—what I wanted was to be included.

How am I putting together the photograph and the physical memory of being bullied? I'd accepted my position as outsider so fully that it seemed to define me, unchangeable, even when I acted as a radical. That speaker in the photo, then, had to be a fraud, feel like a fraud, an imitation of a radical hero.

I remember my colleague Howard Zinn as a true radical hero. It's not a question of his ideas—it's that he was a man of real moral courage. He wasn't trying to impress anyone as a special person. Quietly, generously, he did what he felt needed to be done.

Once, Robert McNamara, Secretary of Defense, was speaking at a hotel in downtown Boston. Along with fifty or so protestors, I lay down on the sidewalk to prevent him from entering. After a while, the police scattered us. Of course, McNamara had already entered the hotel using a back entrance, along with the chair of Howard Zinn's History Department. Howard spoke into a bullhorn. On our walk back to BU, he said, "This is the week I'm up for tenure. Too bad. I really wanted to stay this time."

That very day the History Department had approved him for tenure. But he hadn't known that. By speaking, by blocking the hotel door, he'd risked his career.

I stayed safe.

I was, until I was fifteen, a plump short kid, a year too young for my class. In the shower after gym class, I was one of those whipped by wet towels, jeered at for not having much hair on my groin. Then in one year, when I was sixteen, I grew eight inches and gained no weight; I was suddenly lean and six feet tall. Girls noticed me. I pretended to be the person they saw. But my success felt unreal, a covering-up of my real self, of my weakness.

At Columbia College, again as a day student, I merged into the character of a radical—I learned to play folk guitar, not well, but well enough to accompany songs of freedom. I fought with my father. I wore jeans and tied a red kerchief around my neck. I read Marx. At hootenannies I heard Pete Seeger sing Woody Guthrie's songs, heard Sonny Terry and Brownie McGhee sing and play the blues. At the same time, I began to read poetry and fiction and spend time at Rienzi's in Greenwich Village. It was all about finding, *making*, a new self by merging with others whose identities seemed more firm than my own—radicals, bohemians. I became a radical and a bohemian, a *litterateur*. A romantic outsider. In my final month of undergraduate work, I met a lovely young woman who would become, a couple of months later, my first wife. We took the subway down to City Hall with a couple of friends and married, with clerks as witnesses.

We didn't tell our parents we were married. Until we found an apartment, we lived that way for months, each in our parental home. Then, in our first apartment, we fought. We fought, being so young, so unprepared for marriage. She had lost her father a year before; neither of us had ever lived away from home. She still had one more year at Barnard. I couldn't give her the emotional support or the financial support she needed, and I refused to take financial help from her family. She took help but never let me know.

I worked in an advertising agency as a trainee—mostly as a courier, a mailman. On Madison Avenue one day, lugging a bag of mail, I bumped into a man who'd been a fellow student in a class on Dostoyevsky and Tolstoy. "So, what are your plans?" I asked.

"I've been asking myself what I'd like to do," he said. "And right away I knew—I'd like to stand in front of a class and talk about books."

So random! So strange—what if we didn't happen to meet! I never saw that classmate again. But what he said rang bells. To teach literature and write—why, that would be wonderful. I stayed up all night talking, talking; talking it over with Marilyn. And by the dawn I'd decided to go to graduate school to study literature—and at the same time, to write fiction.

With no preparation for teaching, I taught sixth grade—taught at the same day school I attended as a child. In a year we had a baby, a girl. *Laura.* I was teaching, helping take care of a baby, cooking, giving my undergraduate wife as much help as I could, taking courses at NYU, teaching myself to write. Now I had to swallow my pride, had to take money from parents for rent. My need for help made me feel I was weak—as if I were still that frightened, bullied child, and still didn't want anyone to find me out.

Now I look back and forgive myself, laugh at myself for thinking I was weak, taking for granted all we accomplished. How did we do so much? How did my first wife, eighteen years old when we met and married, finish her degree at Barnard and still take care of a baby? How did we work so hard developing our careers and also bring up a child, raise Laura into the wonderful, creative woman she's become?

***

Let me skip ahead, fast forward, past graduate work at Indiana University—hers in psychology, mine in literature—past my teaching at Victoria College, in Victoria, British Columbia, past a temporary separation—a year in Europe teaching American soldiers for the University of Maryland, then traveling and camping together with Marilyn and Laura for six months before taking a position at Boston University.

Now came the years when I taught in a wonderful program that blended music, art, and literature. I grew close to my students—sharing the experience of the arts and their interrelation—and sharing resistance to the war in Vietnam and the war against people of color. I saw—we saw—the university as oppressive, the government as oppressive. I became "advisor" to SDS—Students for a Democratic Society—though as "advisor" I offered no advice. I just attended dull, rancorous meetings, where resisters tried to show themselves more politically hip, more ideologically correct, than one another, and I tried to seem as if I belonged. I became a member of New University Conference and Resist. I went to demonstrations against the war in New York or D.C.

I protested but stayed safe. And really, what I was most passionate about was literature. I never felt authentic as an ideologue; everything I loved about the arts told me that truth was in complexity, mystery, openness to contradictory ideas. I felt authentic as a teacher of literature, music, and the visual arts. The arts expand consciousness;

ideology constricts, contracts consciousness. In every demonstration I stayed far away from the fighters who yelled "Pigs, pigs," at the police—partly because I knew that what they wanted was trouble and ego inflation, not change. Still, in the late sixties I was a little ashamed of loving and teaching literature and the arts. Wasn't I being self-indulgent when the war in Vietnam was intensifying?

The more I identified as a radical, the less connected I was to my wife. By the fall of 1968, separated from Marilyn, I took an unfurnished two-room apartment in the South End of Boston, repaired but not refurbished, rented from a working man who'd put a lot of sweat equity into his battered brownstone on Dartmouth Street. He intended to rip the walls down and remake the inside. Meantime, what'd he care if I went to work with paper and a staple gun to cover up the dreary green paint? At an outdoor billboard company, I begged overstocked rolls of outdoor billboard sections—landscape from a Volkswagen ad, horses, clowns from a Ringling Brothers Circus billboard—and in my front room I slapped them up in mad combinations, stapled horses' heads beside a clown's face flowing into a brook. Color, plenty of color; the art work in circles of dots of varied saturation: seen up close it became pointillist. Two walls of color and a wall with a window. On the whole fourth wall, above a salvaged door supported on file cabinets for a desk, I glued architectural cork for a bulletin board.

So that was one room; ah, but the other, the other was

its opposite: subdued, romantic—I covered the whole floor with foam rubber, covered the foam with Indian bedspreads and old rugs—so cheap! Indian bedspreads hung over the walls, too, and billowed from the ceiling, and above, tiny colored lights strung, like a starry sky above a tent. It *was* a tent. A stereo in the corner, an unhappy ficus in front of a window that didn't get much light, a brass hookah in the corner. When my eleven-year-old daughter Laura came on Wednesdays and weekends with her baby brother Josh, she watered the ficus and made her bed anywhere in the room.

As far as my students were concerned, or the members of my political action group, or other teachers, I was a hip radical, a little wild, part of youth culture, not academe. I did everything I could to believe I'd created a new, powerful, "righteous" self. The war in Vietnam, the condition of schools for black children in Roxbury, they were real issues, but I myself wasn't real. I became, I *needed* to become, the fictional persona I'd borrowed from the culture—the man whom other people saw but whom I didn't believe.

I'd been with practically no women when I was in college. Marrying so young was my way of escaping my family. But now, alone, I brought many women to my apartment. Somehow, I conflated erotic life with political life. The women I was with, younger than I was, sometimes students, though never my own students, were often political comrades.

I remember one woman, let's call her Lucia. Lean and graceful—we did yoga together once a week at the church in Harvard Square, a church she named, because it leaned slightly, the Church of the Inaccurate Construction. We did yoga, we spent nights together, we did politics. Along with others, we stood once a month in front of the draft board at the corner of Harvard Street and Beacon, and handed out information to the draftees who lined up, six in the morning—information about ways they could avoid going to war. Then, too—politics in the middle of the night: Lucia drove. At the corner, the car stopped, I jumped out and climbed on the hood to paste stickers in big print: "THE WAR" on STOP signs in downtown Boston.

STOP
THE WAR

In that photograph on Commonwealth Avenue, I'm wearing jeans and a dress shirt and jacket. But no tie—as if to indicate that I'm both part of youth culture and am acceding to mid-sixties expectations of respectability. So innocent, so young. I'm no academic professional. Me? I'm a radical hero, model for a new age. I care about my students, care about opening them up; I'm a catalyst of transformation. *Be like me*. It's theater; I'm acting a part I've absorbed from campus radicals.

I'm peddling a false self.

***

In spring, 1968, my cousin—my mother's nephew— calls. I hadn't seen him for fifteen years—not since I was a freshman at Columbia. He's about fifty. I'm thirty-three. His daughter is on a college tour and my cousin wants me to give her the lay of the land at BU. He invites me to dinner at a good restaurant in downtown Boston.

The sommelier comes to our table. My cousin furrows his brow and orders—it's a serious business. *So bourgeois,* I say to myself. My cousin's gray business suit, his evident unease—I see it in his desire to prove to the sommelier that he's a sophisticate. His unease proves he's anything but. *So fucking bourgeois.* Like that. Pronounced *Buh-shwah.* As if to put down all the old farts, prisoners of the culture—which we were all afraid of becoming, and secretly feared, and denied, and knew we were.

The sommelier returns with a bottle; he shows the bottle to my cousin and pours a few drops into a small silver cup hanging from around his neck and tastes, then pours a few more drops into my cousin's wine glass, and my cousin tastes, nods, hands the sommelier a ten-dollar bill for his effort. I judge, I judge. I feel that my cousin is the enemy. He makes a comment about student protest; he announces that it annoys him. "They don't know how good they have it."

So I know which side he's on.

Bourgeois, I say to myself again. Originally referring to someone living in a burg—a town; then referring to a class—it's taken two directions—Marxist and Flaubertian.

In those days I blurred the two, but along with Flaubert I mostly thought of bourgeois as a moral and aesthetic category. To be bourgeois meant to be rich, vulgar, self-centered, pretentious, materialistic. To lack courage and independence. To spend money on comfort and image. To have money and feel you deserve it, use it to keep the world easy to handle.

To hand a sommelier a ten-dollar bill.

I remember my uncle slipping a bill to a headwaiter.

My cousin poured a tiny bit of wine into his daughter's glass; he and I shared the rest.

A little tipsy, I spoke past my respectable cousin to his daughter. I feel it's my duty. I blab. You need to know, I tell the girl, how completely you'll change your life at college the next four years. All the old rules, they'll be tossed away. Oh, sure, you'll have to be careful, but unless you're willing to get past the self you have now, college won't be useful. You're going to make a whole new self, I told her. You're going to break all the rules.

The more I spoke, the more uncomfortable my cousin became. It was as if we were battling for her soul. How arrogant I was! I never heard from him again. She must have been totally bewildered. What was I talking about? I must have sounded like a fool to her. I hope she didn't listen to me. I'm pretty sure she didn't matriculate at BU.

***

The real radical heroes destroyed themselves. I stayed safe.

I think about Jimi Hendrix, his back to his stoned acolytes, on stage at Monterey, screwing his guitar; he gestured furious thumping sex, then smashed the beloved guitar. A crazy sacrifice at a black mass. In just a few years Hendrix would burn out—he himself the sacrifice. For the good children of successful parents, the daemonic was unleashed. Unleashed in Hendrix—and Jim Morrison, "King of Orgasmic Rock"—so it didn't have to be enacted by the good children. Hendrix, Morrison did the dying. And on 11th Street off Fifth in Manhattan, the theater-of-the-self turned real and terrible when explosives blew up the bomb makers along with the townhouse.

Not me. I stood on a wooden box on Commonwealth Avenue, and one of my students or one of my political comrades took a photograph of me, righteous and innocent, smiling, perhaps calling for a student strike.

***

In the fall of 1969, I went to teach at the University of Massachusetts in Amherst. I was glad to get away from politics night after night. But soon, because the war didn't stop, I found myself getting deeply involved again. I was part of a political study group. I got entangled in meetings. We protested the war, I got arrested and jailed at Westover Air Force base. I started, with a friend, the People's Community Union. The PCU included a weekly food co-op, a monthly newspaper of protest, support for migrant workers, and an office where people could read radical literature.

It held together for a year or two, and then gradually dwindled. I wanted it to dwindle. I grew less active politically, stopped needing to prove to myself that I was a radical hero. I put more of myself into my teaching. I wrote more fiction than I had written when I was at BU—wrote stories, began a novel. Under the direction of a carpenter, I built a house. With crow bar, chain saw, and a come-along, we pulled down an old tobacco barn in order to salvage the boards, used the old, weathered boards as paneling for the new house. I was a city kid—I didn't know how to hammer a nail. By the time the house was finished, I'd grown a little more capable and a lot stronger.

Gradually, that false self, that fierce, innocent, would-be hero of the photograph, has morphed into someone else—someone more honest, more aware of the comedy of the false self. Sometimes I don't recognize him. Sometimes I'll hear myself talking—say to a friend, or talking in a group, or talking to my wife, Sharon, and it will flash across my mind: Who is this person talking? Interesting. Look at what I've become. Somehow, I've grown closer to *being* a self by not trying to be a self.

At the restaurant, I'd told my cousin's daughter—my second cousin—she'd have to make herself over. But of course, *I* was the one who had to do that—not to construct a self but to give up my own false self. I'm still—in my eighties—in process.

***

Here's what I'm not. I'm not the one struggling to become

an authentic self—a boy, lacking a grounding in the turmoil of a childhood family, bullied and fearful at school; a man, holding on to ideology or a bohemian style to give him wholeness—false, false. But it's okay that it's false, because I'm not *him*—I'm the one who *writes about* that boy, that man. In fact, maybe that's why I've written in the first place. I can stand outside the self, above the self, looking down. Ah, that poor slob going through his grief, conflicts, depressions—I can step back from him, float up, stay above, as the writer, the artist. He frees me.

In most of my writing life I've told stories in third person—as *he, him,* Ben, David, Joseph—selves which are at a remove; and even if I've used first person, that speaker isn't *me*—he's distant from myself, an imagined "I," not actually *me.*

But then—I can't trust the writer either, can I? He's become a second self, observing, composing— a self who pretends to be in charge and can look with sympathy and understanding at the one who longs and struggles. I stay safe. My characters release me; they are me and not me, they are simpler and more whole than I am. A reader asks, "Is this story autobiographical?" Even when an event in one of my stories has occurred, the character—Ben, David, Michael—isn't me. And the drama has been simplified, given shape.

This book is as close to my personal truth as I can make it.

Yet even here, there's unease, falsity, in my position

as writer. As soon as I claim that position, as soon as I receive its bounty, a pirate treasure, I feel uncomfortable, knowing what the position does for me. I put on the skin of my character; I hide inside that skin. I play the artist, knowing the role is protection, is also false. Stepping back, I examine and doubt myself. And don't I doubt the one doubting? And back and back: it's turtles all the way down.

NINE

A Nervous Stomach

My mother initially took me to see Dr. Schiff because my stomach was "nervous." She must have suspected that the high-pitched howling in my stomach—as if I were on a roller coaster or in a plane suddenly dropping—arose from the terrible fights, fights almost every night—I've written so often about the fights—my father shouting, my mother cursing him in an English that had the feeling of her home language. *My blood is black, black is my blood,* then slamming shut the windows—"so the neighbors won't hear"—but actually so he'd feel shame. Furious, he jerked them open again. I knew, even at five or six or ten, that she wanted him to goad her to the next level of ugliness.

You can't order me *to shut up,* he yelled.

You animal, you stupid, crude animal.

Each the other's victim.

***

One evening, only once, a neighbor did knock on the door—"Excuse, mister, my child is sleeping. Can you please be a little more quiet?"—and my father—two hundred pounds of uncomprehending shame and rage, slammed the door, and, through the door, cursed the man: "you—you goddamn refugee!"

My mother never let him forget this. "Shh, shh!" she'd whisper, "a little more quiet or we'll have the 'goddamn refugee' at the door"— but actually *wanting* him to yell, yell at her, yell at me. *Let the wild rumpus start.*

He wasn't a hitter. All he did was yell. All he did was shove her into the bedroom and slam the door, leave her in solitary for the evening. I'd retreat to my bedroom. He stood outside my door. "You! It's all your fault, you little bum!"

But the waiting for the nightly fight to begin, that was worse—electric air before a storm. A relief when the thunder came. He bellowed—what about?—the length of my hair, the starch in his shirts, my mother's cigarettes. But mostly money. "Come on, big boy, you want to fight?" she asked, putting up her fists.

She was, he said, "a goddamn spendthrift. You're bringing the kid up to be a bum. Want him to think money grows on trees? You, you're bleeding me!"

"Be careful, my dear. Did you know the 'kid' you speak of happens to be in the room?" She pretended to placate a monster, "Whatever you say, my dear, you must be right if you grunt so loudly. Yes, if you want to label me a spendthrift, *fine,* but remember your son."

So, he yelled louder. Now, as if her defenses had collapsed, all the charm, all the contempt, she feigned fainting, as if stunned, a cow at the slaughterhouse hit with a hammer. Her eyes were blank and rolling. Gaga. Her mouth hung open.

It was terrible, terrible each night, full of pain. But also . . . comic. It made me giggle—the stages were so fixed, predetermined. And now it was time to go all-in: she dug her nails into the skin of her upper arm till the blood came. She smeared the blood on her housecoat. And now it was time for Yiddish. In Yiddish she turned into a different creature—not the gracious, cultured matron she saw herself mornings after he had gone to work—my delightful mother—but a mad, hunched crone spitting curses in rhythmic Yiddish, flailing her nails at his face.

I retreated to my bedroom to play music on my wind-up record player.

Later, middle of the night, I'd wake to see her in housecoat standing at the door to my room, smoking, watching me sleep, unable to sleep herself. I was afraid of her madness but—knowing how much she loved me—I was ashamed to be afraid, to imagine her burning up the house or doing something terrible with a knife. Yet didn't she, many times, get on her knees in front of the oven and stick her head in? Didn't she pretend to hunt for poison in the medicine cabinet? "Say—which do you think will do the job?"

"So, my son and heir," she whispered. How's your stomach? Better tonight?"

"Okay." Not so okay. "Better."

"Go back to sleep."

"*You* go back to sleep."

"Shh. We'll talk in the morning."

***

We went to see Dr. Schiff.

It was a time before medical insurance. You got a bill; you paid. My mother had a different opinion. Imagine her a princess who had to flee a revolution but expected tradesmen and professionals to treat her—and therefore her son—as special. She wasn't begging; it was her due. So, *nu,* if she wasn't a princess, she was at least a great lady. For me, she *was* a great lady. But the contradiction between great lady and nightmare crone was bewildering. How were they the same person? Was she putting on an act?

Which was the act?

We'd go to "the best specialist in New York." After seeing the doctor, and being approached by his receptionist with the bill, my mother smiled and waved it away. "My dear," she said, "I *never* pay full price. I pay, *au plus,* ten dollars." It was as if she felt embarrassed for the poor receptionist for not understanding.

She always got away with it.

But with Dr. Schiff things were a little different.

We took a taxi through Central Park, West side to the East side. She wore her beautiful, gray silk suit, and I was dressed in shirt, tie and blazer. In his examination room the doctor asked me questions. Dr. Schiff had a long, handsome face, a shining bald skull, and, speaking in his deep voice, emanated power that didn't need to assert itself. From the first he took to me as I to him. Oh, did I play up to him! Oh, did my mother play up to him! Outside our happy home she became gracious, charming, beautiful.

He was in his fifties, she in her forties.

After his examination of me—I'm imagining it was mostly questions about my life—he told me to sit in the waiting room while he spoke to my mother. What was he saying to her? The waiting room was full, but Dr. Schiff and my mother remained in his consulting room for what seemed a long time. When they came out, he shook my hand. The receptionist handed my mother a bill. She tried out her usual: "But my dear, I never pay full price . . ."

Dr. Schiff, standing nearby, turned to her. "That's something I decide."

"Oh! I'm so sorry," she said.

"You don't need to worry about a bill," he said.

She was quiet in the taxi. There were tears on her cheeks which she dabbed with a handkerchief. She wanted me to see the tears. "He understands my life," she said.

After this, for a couple of years, when I got sick, Dr. Schiff came to the apartment. My mother was embarrassed at its ordinariness, its lack of elegance. It was an elevator building, but the walls of the elevator were scratched in curses. Still, the apartment was neat, the furniture from Sloan's. She carried her ragged flag aloft. She served him tea.

Sometimes we went to see him at his office. Why? What could he do? But I didn't mind. I remember one visit, one "check-up." Afterwards, as we settled into our seats in the taxi, my mother said, "So, how do you like our Dr. Schiff?"

"A lot. I like him a lot."

"And how would you like him to be your father?"

I peered at her to see if she were playing with me. Her face was solemn. "A lot, a lot! Really, Mom, did he say something? Did he want that? Do it, Mom. It's so awful with you and Dad."

How old was I? Seven, eight? Old enough to understand a lot. My father was out of town. For several months a year, when I was five, six, seven, my father took the train to L.A. and took care of his father. His boss, my uncle, paid his salary. My mother had no one to fight with. It left her depressed. I knew he was "out on the coast" to get away from us. When my mother asked about Dr. Schiff, a door opened in a wall. "Really, Mom?"

"I could go back to work," she said. "Old man Bonwit asked me."

"You could. You *could*. You used to make lots of money."

"But *no*," she said. "That's not what a good Jewish wife and mother does."

"Please, Mom? Please!" I could feel the door closing. "Did he really ask you?"

"Did you think your mother is only the drab frump you see every day? Well?"

"No. No."

"But," she sighed, "what would happen to your poor father?"

I didn't answer.

"I've written him. I told him that if he doesn't come home this month, we won't be there when he gets back. We won't. We'll move to a hotel."

"And what about Dr. Schiff?"

"We'll see."

My father came home the following week. We met him at Grand Central walking toward us up the red carpet they rolled out when the Twentieth Century Limited came in. My suntanned Daddy! I forgot Dr. Schiff. I loved my father, I was hungry to see him.

By the time we were home he was picking on me. My hair too long, my new clothes too expensive . . . .

"Such nice weather," my mother said in elegant accent, as she often spoke when she couldn't bear him.

***

Toward the end of their lives together there was peace in the house. I was foolish enough to mention it. "It's wonderful. You're not screaming at each other, Mom. You seem so peaceful together." My father sat with us in the living room, my little girl riding his knee. He beamed at me.

"Screaming?" she said. "What are you talking about?"

My father's skin sagged on his face. He was so depleted. He had lost thirty or forty pounds; I stared. He spoke in a soft voice. "You're A-1 okay in my book," he said out of the blue. The voice of an "American sport." Now, putting my daughter down, moving as if he were made of glass and afraid to break, he stood outside the bathroom, rocking, rocking, listening down into himself, not wanting to leave our visit but afraid to miss the moment when he might be able to move his bowels.

"Screaming?" my mother whispered again. "What's wrong with you? Don't you know we've had a wonderful marriage, your father and I? Everybody has an occasional disagreement, my dear son. Just look at him—the poor soul wouldn't know what to do without me."

***

He died first—fell "like a tree. He never knew what was happening. Some gentle souls have special deaths. God felled him. I called your uncle. He'll take care of everything. Your poor father's body is already gone to Riverside Memorial Chapel."

"I'll be with you by this evening, Mom. Are you okay?"

"Your uncle will sit with me for a while. I covered the mirrors. The man from the chapel brought me a memorial candle. It burns a whole week."

When I got there from Boston, she was alone. The funeral was to take place the next day. A small funeral. His brother and sister would be there. My parents had few friends. Instead of friends and family, she had candles—not just the seven-day memorial candle but a collection of 24-hour memorial glasses lit on the table—the table where, almost half a century later, I'm writing this. For decades writing this. The living room was full of light.

"You made each other so unhappy," I said. "You don't remember?"

"Nonsense. Your father and I loved each other. I was a happy wife and mother."

I ignored this. "Maybe," I said, "it was largely my fault,"

"You? You were our pride and joy."

We sat on the couch facing the table full of candles. "It's beautiful, the light," she said. "When my little sister died of consumption, when my father and then my mother died, we had candles. By the light, we remember."

Or choose not to remember. I put my memories on a shelf in a closet. Most of my life I've been visiting that shelf. I *remember*. I remember her eyes, the cow in the slaughterhouse stunned with the hammer. I remember her in stained housecoat, middle of the night, standing at the door to my room, smoking. I remember her turning on the gas and putting her head in the oven. But I remember, too, my mother sitting at her 1917 Underwood, typing stories I'd dictate to her as I strode back and forth in their bedroom. I remember her ability to make the world come alive, funny and charming. I'm left with sorrow for her loss of that world—sorrow for our irretrievable losses.

* * *

TEN

The Aunts

GROWING UP AN ONLY CHILD, I had two aunts who competed for my affection—Aunt Ceal, my mother's older sister, who was married but had no children, and Aunt Ann, Ann Jean, my father's younger sister—Nanny-Nan—who was single. Aunt Ann was a lawyer and editor. She graduated law school in Chicago, passed the bar in California, Illinois, and New York, but, as far as I know, didn't practice. During World War II she was editor of a national magazine, a position she lost when the men came back from war. She barely made a living as a free-lance editor. My rich uncle Lloyd, her brother, paid her rent.

Even when she had a demanding job, Nanny-Nan took the time to be my teacher. She spent a lot of time with me, sat me down on a park bench and taught me to read, taught me to do arithmetic. If I grew fidgity, she put her legs across my lap to pin me down. As I got older, sitting on that bench, she gave me problems in logic or ethics, or we read books to each other (*Black Beauty, Great*

Expectations) or got excited about words—she loved roots and cognates and lugged a fat dictionary to the park.

More important, her clarity and calm saved me from the craziness in my family. When I complained, she laid out rational arguments: why I needed to accept it and be a peacemaker.

Aunt Ceal was less intelligent and uneducated, but warmer, more passionate. When I was very young, I loved her to put me to bed and sing to me. She wore loose, romantic clothes and let her black hair grow long. When I was four, she went off to California and returned to New York a year later with a husband and with her hair short and colored red-blonde. She had fallen for a handsome Hungarian, an aristocrat according to his framed coat of arms. Then Alex had an automobile accident that left him brain damaged. Ceal married him anyway.

Returning to New York with her new, damaged husband, she became a different Aunt Ceal. But she was still passionate, still angry, especially about rights of the underdog. She'd herself been an underdog—as a twelve-year-old she fled with her family to America from a little town near Kishinev after the 1903 and 1905 pogroms. She and my mother and their family had been given refuge in the basement of a Russian general. Ceal was three years older—old enough to understand the consequences if they were attacked. Her name had been Czarna or Charne; it became Ceal Kaufman—*Kaufman* the name the family took in America. Then, as a designer, she changed her name to Ceal Kay—her changing names maybe an expression of trauma—of hiding, though everyone knew that she was a Jew.

Trauma internalized as anger.

She couldn't stand the bosses she designed dresses for, and the bosses couldn't stand her. "Those lousy capitalists," she'd snap. "The stinking, lousy bosses—all greedy lice." In the 1940s, when I was growing up, she had a series of jobs—designing a line of dresses for good houses. The firms' owners used her designs, kept the designs she'd made for the following season, but when she fought with them, when she "told them off," they let her go.

Sometimes both aunts came over on a Sunday evening and we listened on the big living room radio to a Fireside Chat. My mother got tears in her eyes—"Just listen to his beautiful voice—listen!"—and sighed. I *did* listen. That sweet, powerful voice of an American King David.

My mother's sister Ceal would be disgusted: "Your Mr. Roosevelt, oh, my yes, such a lovely man. So tell me this—what has he done to save the Jews? Or support striking workers? You know what your wonderful Mr. Roosevelt cares about?—the war profits of General Motors."

My mother rolled her eyes to show contempt. "My sister is so smart. She knows all about politics." They'd snip at each other, my mother and Aunt Ceal. Nanny-Nan—Aunt Ann— would try to make peace.

She never argued; she asked questions. "I know, Ceal, you care a lot about ordinary people, and that's the wonderful thing about you. Can you think of any time Roosevelt cared about ordinary people but had forces pitted against him? Or do you think he's purely evil?"

"I didn't say that."

"No, I know you didn't. Tell me—do you think we want the same kind of world? You, me, your sister Leah, and Mr. Roosevelt?"

Of course, while Aunt Ann played the role of peacemaker and Aunt Ceal the role of righteous defender of the oppressed, there was a more subtle battle going on underneath—for my affection among the three women. Aunt against aunt, my mother against both. My father retreated to the kitchen to wash dishes and listen to the radio.

My mother and my Aunt Ceal would continue to squabble. Sometimes Aunt Ann would shut her eyes. I tried to stay out of it.

***

I see my Aunt Ann now in mind's eye more sharply than I can see my mother. Aunt Ann wore, almost always, a modest, gray, silk shantung suit, Chinese pendant at the collar. I can still smell the peculiar old-spinster odor of that outfit—a bit of cologne, a bit of cleaning fluid, the stale air of her hotel closet—though when I was a child she wasn't old. Maybe forty in 1940, child of the century. Her hair—fine hair, black forever, even when she was fifty and sixty—was rolled into two stiff buns at the sides of her head. From time to time she'd pat the buns. This was hardly *hair*; it was like a wimple or part of a uniform. I never, never saw her hair loosened, not even at the beach. She seems to me a sort of nun—calm, restrained, severe about her own life but very kind, always trying to mollify, to sweeten the atmosphere, eliminate conflict. A Jewish nun? Hardly Jewish, though she'd grown up in a Yiddish-speaking household.

During the war or just after, she became a Rosicrucian; it was as a Rosicrucian she'd talk to me about God and mysteries of the spirit.

"That stuff's not real, I think."

"You *think*, Jackie? Why is it for all these centuries people have imagined God?"

"It makes them feel better. You don't really believe in God, do you, Aunt Ann?"

She didn't try to make me a believer. But she taught me to imagine a mystery, to sense a world we could only partly understand through perception and reason. Which is surprising, since she was such a rationalist.

Socratic questioning was her method.

Aunt Ann lived alone in a residential hotel around the corner on Central Park West. Sometimes I'd go over to her apartment to complain about my father, who'd yelled at me or shoved me into my bedroom. I chose to get sympathy from Ann, not from my Aunt Ceal. I knew Ceal would comfort me, side with me, call my mother and get into a quarrel— but then I'd see myself as the victim.

Aunt Ann would make me into the strong one; she would give me strength.

I'm putting this episode together out of many episodes. Who knows, after all this time, what words we used? But here's the way things were.

Even in her own apartment she wore the gray suit. Her apartment was small but uncluttered. No—it was bare. Her tiny office she kept closed. In the main room—her bedroom-living room—I remember a polished table, two chairs, plain gold drapes, lamps on end tables, a day bed, and over the day bed a print of something—maybe a landscape. She offered me a slice of whole wheat bread and butter, carrots, a glass of Walker Gordon raw (unpasteurized) milk.

"I know for a fact your father loves you. He means well, dear, but unfortunately he isn't very smart," she said. "He was always a good boy, protecting his brother and me. He always took care of his parents. He's 100% loyal. But—not so smart. So, what does that tell you? Jackie? Tell me. Who is it who can bring peace into the house?"

"My mother?"

"Your mother is very smart, but can she soften him? What do you think?"

"No." I was caught up in Aunt Ann's rhythm. "No."

"Then who else in that house can be the smart one?" Aunt Ann looked around the room as if to seek out all the possible candidates. She sat beside me, poked my chest with her forefinger. To poke—I realize now—was for Aunt Ann an act of tenderness. She rarely hugged, never gave me lipstick kisses like my mother or Aunt Ceal. She poked.

"Anyone but you? Don't *you* have to be the smart one?" She poked. Taking my hand, she asked God for a blessing for all of them—for my mother, my father, for me.

"Now," Aunt Ann said, in lawyerly tones, "Let's make a list. What can you think of doing that will make him feel less frightened?"

"Dad? Frightened?"

"Jackie! Don't you *know* how frightened he is? How out to sea? Your poor father. And frightened of *you*, because he's not very smart and you are."

"You think he's stupid? He runs a bunch of salesmen, doesn't he?"

"Especially not so smart in the heart. I love your father. But if you don't help, what's going to happen?"

"Maybe he'll leave. Or maybe my mom will leave."

"That's right. You're a smart boy. Wouldn't you want to be able to prevent such a thing?"

No! No, I wouldn't. But I couldn't say that. In the rhetorical game she'd created, such a wish didn't belong. Only gestures of reconciliation were acceptable.

"Let's make a list," she said. Aunt Ann found a legal pad and a pencil. "Let's list strategies that will make him less frightened."

I began a list. "I need to apologize." Then: "I need to stay out of his way."

"Dear? What about this—another way: You need to show you respect him even when you don't. You might try . . . to admire him, the way you just did—as a salesman. Ask him about selling. Ask him how he goes about it."

The list went on. I see now that the list was shaped mostly by my aunt, strategies to soothe my bear of a father.

I was to get a haircut even if I didn't want one.

I was to ask my father to go to Central Park with me and have a catch, "even if you don't care about having a catch."

I put that on the list, not telling her how Dad yelled when I dropped the ball.

"You understand," Aunt Ann said, "I'm his sister, and I know what a fool he can be. Being in the right isn't going to get you anywhere. He's not going to change. He's of the old school. So. Will you try?"

"Sure." As victor I could make allowances for my foolish father.

Of course, my father wasn't all that unaware. He knew he was seen by his own son as a dummy that required handling. And my strategy couldn't change the way my mother smothered me with little presents—a set-up if ever there was one.

For instance, a book. My mother would buy me a book, say *The Old Man and the Sea,* put it at my place at the table, and my father would get annoyed. "What's this?

Another present? How much did that goddamn book cost you?"

"When you learn to read, you'll understand," she'd sigh, using her best stage-English accent—though she knew my father could read; he read the newspaper every day. He grew silent and his heavy shoulders hunched up; in this posture he was dangerous. He'd bellow at me in his army voice, "You see? You little bastard—you cause all the trouble around here."

Sometimes I played the role Aunt Ann scripted. I'd bow my head and wouldn't answer, or I'd say "Sorry, sorry, Dad." And the rage would blow over. But sometimes I'd talk back: "Oh, I'm so terrible. I read books. It's all my fault."

And my father would bellow, "You—you snotty little bastard. What kind of a boy are you?"

I'd leave the table. He'd get up and push me into my room. I locked the door—that way I could curse him, and he couldn't reach me. It made us both safe.

***

Aunt Ann came over once or twice a week. She was no cook; alone, she ate raw eggs heated up under the hot-water tap, slices of whole wheat bread, raw vegetables. She drank carrot and celery juice made with a stainless-steel juicer, her only extravagance. She was a food nut half a century before it became the rage.

"When she comes for dinner, that's the only time she has a real meal," my father laughed. My father, my mother, laughed at Aunt Ann. "She thinks she knows everything, but let me tell you . . . ."

Sometimes when she came over, she corralled her brother, my father, stood him up against the wall and poked. She poked, and Dad chuckled and grinned, turning his head side to side to escape her message about sugar and white flour, about whole milk. Or about him and me. No escape—and no defenses against his smart sister.

He'd grin and flush and chuckle. She'd whisper to him. Sometimes I knew the whispering was about me, about a fight she'd seen at the table. After Ann left, Dad would say, "You and me, we got to try to be decent. What do you say?"

For a while there'd be peace in the house. It wouldn't last. I remember an episode repeated in one form or another again and again. I was about fifteen. My father, hunched over his checkbook, a monthly trial for all of us, yelled, "TURN OFF THAT GODDAMN FUNERAL MUSIC—I'M TRYING TO PAY MY BILLS!" Classical music, which I had begun listening to, partly as a defense against my father, was all "funeral music" to him.

"Nice!" my mother said. "Refined, don't you think so, Jack?"

I hunched my head forward, puffed out my lips, mimed a baboon scratching his chest.

This was meant not to be seen by my father, or to be so minimal a gesture it could be denied. I'd gotten away with it before. But Dad spotted it and bolted up from his desk, scattering papers, and the mess inflamed him still more. "You get in your room, you mama's boy, or I'll beat the crap out of you."

What a snotty kid I was! I feel now more compassion for that poor, humiliated man than for the smug little oedipal victor using classical music as a way of asserting his superiority! We were both of us humiliated—I, terrified by raw male power, my father ashamed that his son was smarter than he, enraged that his wife and son were ganging up against him once again.

By the time I was in my teens, Aunt Ann came less often for dinner, finally explaining, "You know, dear I can't take the pain I see in that house. I come for you—but it's hard."

One night there was a particularly terrible fight. My mother called Aunt Ann—something she never did. My father ripped the phone out of the wall—something he did when my mother talked too long or talked about *him*. Ann came over to mollify, to calm the waters. My father went for a walk. My mother closed herself in their bedroom. Ann and I were left sitting on the bed in my room.

"Now, listen, Jack. I'm very serious. I don't want to see you damaged. A life like this will damage you. There's no question. I know what I went through as a child. I know what it did to me. Do you know what your grandfather was like?"

"I don't remember him much."

"Your father was beaten almost every day by your

grandfather. Not your uncle Lloyd, not me. Your father was the oldest. If the slightest thing your father did bothered your grandfather, out came the strap. That's all he knew. Has your father every hit you?"

"No."

"I remember when our parents had to take in a boarder, and your father took the last piece of stew meat at dinner, not waiting for the boarder to take seconds. Our father didn't even yell. He pulled off his belt and whipped your father across the cheek. It left a welt. Your father left the table. I looked all over for him. Then I heard him under the stairs, weeping."

She took a pad from her bag, made a line down the middle, and handed me the pencil. "Now, I want a list."

"A list? What I'd tell him if he wasn't such a moron?"

"Subjunctive: *weren't.*"

"If he *weren't* such a moron?"

"He's not a moron. But that's right—a list."

I began, and within a few minutes I'd covered the column and given Aunt Ann the pad. But no. "You read it aloud," she said. I did.

"How does that sound?"

"Like a crybaby. Now what?"

"Can't you guess? On the right column, write what your father feels. How can he be as terrible as that father in the left column and still believe he's a good person. And he does, you know. He wants to be good. So what would he say?"

And I wrote. When my father came home (was this in the evening, was this on a Sunday morning?—I don't remember) Aunt Ann took her brother into the kitchen. They talked. I heard him weeping, as in Aunt Ann's story about the belt and the boarder. I'd never heard him cry. I went into the kitchen to apologize. I hugged my father.

***

After my father died and my mother moved to a sweet little apartment around the corner on Central Park West, she felt her life was complete. She'd had, she was convinced, a very good marriage. "But," she asked, "why don't you call me? If I give you money for the phone, would you call?"

I called—but not enough. I visited—but not enough. Sometimes she called me and, when I picked up, she didn't speak, just breathed heavily into the phone. "Mom?"

"This is a call from the cemetery."

"Oh, Mom."

But once, when she called me, it was to say that my Aunt Ceal had had a stroke. My mother and I found places for Ceal and Alex in a nursing home. I came into the city to see my Aunt Ceal. Sitting in her wheel chair in the middle of a big room, once a gym loft, she was like a wrinkled tiny puppet. All around, clatter and cries of the old people. Aunt Ceal was filled with rage—against the food, against the *shwartze*—the lovely black woman from Jamaica who took care of her. "I'm so sorry," I said. "My aunt . . ."

"She's just a poor sick old lady," the woman said. "She don't mean it. She don't know what she's saying."

Ceal hardly recognized me. She screamed, screamed at the attendant. "Look who's taking care of me!"

A month later she was dead.

***

Once, when I was in the city visiting my mother, Ann called and came by to see my mother, not to see me. She hardly spoke to me, hardly looked at me. I knew she'd renounced our connection. Though she'd been so important, so necessary to me, we'd lost each other; I felt ashamed. It was my fault. I saw her as restrictive, old fashioned, while I was trying to make myself radically new. From the time I graduated college and moved out of my parents' apartment, I'd paid almost no attention to my aunts.

Ann was physically so strong. She saw herself as a walking proof of her exercise and diet. I remember racing her on the beach one summer when I was about fifteen—she could outrun me easily. She used to claim that she'd live to 120. But this Sunday morning, she was visiting my mother because she was worried about her health and wanted advice. Something was wrong with her stomach. My mother said, "It's because you don't eat right." She suggested that Ann try—I can't remember what.

But I do remember that Ann actually listened to my mother, took her suggestions seriously. As she listened, I had a chance to look at Aunt Ann's face—at her eyes, the dark bags under her eyes. She was dressed in the same gray suit I remembered, but the clothing sagged; she'd lost weight.

When she was leaving, I kissed Aunt Ann's cheek and remembered the scent I'd known so well, and knew she'd surely given up on me. I promised myself I'd call her, write her, visit her. I did call, but we had little to say to each other.

After she left that morning, my mother sighed. "She doesn't look so good, does she. Let's hope she doesn't have anything terrible."

At the end of her lease, Ann moved to a retirement apartment in Florida, and I never saw her again—because she *did* have something terrible. In a few months she was dead. My mother called me up and in Yiddish told me about Ann, as if such things should be given the full weight of her childhood language—or as if to announce it in clear English were too dangerous. And then she added in a whisper, "*Fershtayste,* my son? It's finished. It's all over. You understand me?"

I understood and didn't understand. Now I understand.

ELEVEN

Waiting for Polly Adler

IT'S SUNDAY MORNING, sun barely up over the sea; it's early summer, we're in Long Beach, Long Island, and it's 1927, so Long Beach is kind of chic, with huge, white stucco houses and expensive hotels that by the time I was born had come down in the world. And my uncle, Lloyd Clayton is maybe thirty, thirty-one, killer-handsome, not yet rich but getting there fast, and he's waiting in bed in the best hotel in Long Beach for Polly Adler, madam of the most successful whorehouse in New York, to close up shop and drive out from the city to meet him for a convivial Sunday. His Stetson hat, mirrored in the pink morning light from the mirror over the dresser, is hanging on a clothes caddy that holds his white linen suit, his two-tone brown/white sporty shoes. He can't sleep. He's been unable to sleep all night.

I know about this from long talks, early 1970s, when he was in his mid-seventies and I was in my thirties. Or not so much talks: he talked, I listened. Why did I listen? He was so toxic in my life, this man in the lives of my parents. Somehow, though I hated him, when he needed a listener, I was there.

He loved to recount the stories of his youth, the Story of his Youth. We'd walk along Central Park South, both of us hot-shot walkers who loved gobbling up sidewalk. I remember being amazed by the way young women would turn their heads to look at him, not at me—Uncle Lloyd in his cashmere coat and that brushed felt Stetson. When I imagine that morning in Long Beach waiting for Polly Adler, I'm inventing the Stetson hanging on that hook on the clothes caddy, because I can't remember Uncle Lloyd without his hat. In the picture above my desk, his beautiful head of hair, wavy, silver ever since he was in his late twenties, is hatless, but the perfect Stetson is in his hand. He's just lifted it off for the snapshot in front of his black 1934 sixteen-cylinder Cadillac. Phony grin. Click. Dressed in crisp white shirt, beige linen slacks and two-tone shoes, he stands on Riverside Drive squeezing the shoulder of his "Pop," my grandfather who died when I was eight, a little man with a brushy white moustache, a tough little man who beat his children with a belt.

It was a pale gray Stetson, not a cowhand's hat but something an oil tycoon or a cattle baron might wear, or the Governor of a Western state. He'd become a Westerner at home "in the concrete canyons," a wealthy sport with a big racetrack watch—every year he'd take the Hudson River Day Line and then the train up to Saratoga for racing season. He didn't want you to think he was old-money,

East-coast American; he was gaudy spirit from the West and spoke with movie-Western accent—though he'd grown up in Chicago, and the only "West" he knew was Palm Springs, California, where he eventually settled my grandfather. Always on stage, his voice resonant, he sustained his vowels, let them echo through his chest, as if he were a cantor chanting Torah.

This is about a self-made, rich American. Born poor, he made himself *rich;* born the son of a Russian-Jewish immigrant, Yiddish his first language, he made himself *American,* a man-about-town in prohibition New York, acquaintance of Mickey Walker, His Dis-honor the Mayor, pal of the Police chief. What was it, when he was growing up, that let him see past the models of adulthood around him? After all, he was born poor in Chicago, 1898, born Louis Cohon—his father (my grandfather) a rebellious Jew from Odessa. You hear stories of Jews tossing overboard their tefillin when they passed the Statue of Liberty; my grandfather had discarded all such trappings years before he came to America. By the time I knew Grandpa, just before World War II, he'd discarded Yiddish. "I'm as American as Uncle Sam," he loved saying in heavily-accented English. My grandfather never looked back. Later, if you asked my father or my uncle about their history, they'd say in exactly the same words, "Ahh, what do you want to hear that old-time crap for?"

Old-time crap meant anything before Uncle Lloyd's rise to glory. Meant history. As far as he was concerned, the world before he started fighting it, climbing it, didn't matter one bit. He was sure that's what America was all about—dumping the way things used to be. Starting fresh. But the rise itself, oh, that he loved to talk about. We'd be walking past the Plaza Hotel and he'd grab my arm and point up to the green-streaked copper mansard roof as if it were challenging or confirming his power, and he'd say, "When I first came to this burg, I'd walk these concrete canyons and yell up there, 'You don't scare me one damn bit. I'm the boy for you. You watch. I'll have you eating out of my hand.' And didn't I do all right? You bet your ass."

So Uncle Lloyd made himself up. *Lloyd Clayton*: much too phony a name, and if in 1919, coming out of the Army, he'd been a little more sophisticated, as he was just a few years later, he'd have changed *Louis Cohon* less obviously. But that's the point: he learned so fast—but had such a lot to learn. What was he, after all, but the youngest son of greenhorns from Russia, poor as hell, his old man a Jewish atheist, angry socialist who worked in a loft in Chicago rolling cigars, his mother a terrorized, submissive woman who took in boarders? He'd graduated eighth grade, Louis Cohon, and that was the best any of the brothers could do. His younger sister, such a smart girl, Ann Cohon, not only went on to high school; she eventually put herself through college and law school—but the three boys took jobs after seventh grade or after eighth. That's how they could afford to keep Ann in school.

There are people who parlay advantage into advantage. He worked all day in a stockroom; then, saving the nickel carfare, he walked to downtown Chicago to study. His salary went to his mother—but he kept back enough to pay for classes. At fourteen, my uncle learned stenography, then court stenography, and by fifteen, pretending to be older, he was working at a Chicago courthouse. Everything proceeded from that. But suppose it hadn't been stenography—wouldn't he have found another way?

It was the stenography that, when the army needed men who could take dictation and type, gave Louis—still "Louis" in 1917—entrée to a commission; made an officer straight from civilian life, he lived in Washington in officers' quarters and was secretary to a general. And that's where he must have learned a smattering of manners, of proper English. Because how could he have learned to speak so well among poor kids in the public schools of Chicago?

By 1923, Lloyd was making a lot of money as a tire salesman in New York. He was already a young man about town. Yet he was shy with women, scared of women—fifty years later he laughed at "what a pusillanimous fellow I was. You didn't know I could use ten-dollar words like *pusillanimous*, did you?" He went to Polly Adler's not for the girls but for the talk, for the laughs. It's where the big shots hung out. And he liked Polly, and "she made a big fuss over me."

But when he got to New York right out of the Army, he had no job, no friends. He used to brag about how he got the job selling. He was staying in a cheap rooming house on the West side, pinching pennies while he looked for work. And he thought to himself, *Here I am in a brand-new world. We own this sonofabitch world. There ain't no country like this country.* He knew enough by the time he told me this story not to use "sonofabitch," not to use "ain't." In fact, he was vain about his "grammar" and "ten-dollar words." But he loved the panache of that tough-guy language.

"You'd think it was a cinch, wouldn't you, getting a job after the war. But see, the economy hadn't kicked in. Guys on their knees for jobs, took what they could get, the poor bastards. And I said to myself, *what are these shmucks gonna need? Where can I get in on the ground floor?"* So he took his sweet time, squeezing the time from his war bonus, from his savings, living stingy in that rooming house. How many soldiers came home from that war with money saved up? He looked at ads, he read the papers.

"Then one day, I got dressed up in my only suit, and I walked into a store—where they sold tires. I'd been casing the joint. Plate glass window, bare linoleum floor, tires sitting on little wooden stands, a brand-new store sign in the window. And I asked for a job. 'What do you know about tires?' the boss asked. He was a hard-assed guy. *I* was a hard-assed guy. "'Not a goddamn thing,' I told him, 'but I'm a smart guy and a good salesman.' And I could see his eyes staring past me—he was thinking how to get rid of me politely and maybe three other things at the same time—and I said to him, 'Look here. Just try me out. Next guy who walks through that door, try me out. If I make the sale, you give me a job.' 'But you don't know tires,' he says. 'I will when you spend five minutes and explain.' Well, right there I had the sonofabitch, because I had him investing in me, you get what I mean?"

It could have gone lousy—he admitted that later on—but as soon as he saw the man he had to sell, he knew he'd be all right. It was a little man with a swagger. "The combination," Lloyd said, "was unbeatable." Five minutes, he had a hand on the guy's shoulder and hush-hush, as if it had to be kept from the boss, he was offering him the best deal in the store—only of course it wasn't the best deal, it wasn't a deal at all.

"'I guess you've got yourself a job,' the boss said to me. 'I'll start you off at $25 a week—right after the training period.' Now, twenty-five a week was a damned good salary those days. Better than the most money my pop ever made. Here's what I told him: 'I want fifty dollars a week.'

"Ridiculous! I knew I'd never get it just like that. 'Here's the deal,' I told him. 'I work for you for six months at twenty-five bucks, and then if you think I'm worth it, you pay me in back-wages the other twenty-five bucks for the whole six months, starting today—or you don't, fine!—I walk out, no hard feelings. What d'you got t'lose?'"

Six months later—of course, because it's that kind of story—the boss was glad to pay him back wages of $25 additional a week. In another year, with commission, he was earning $10,000. By 1925 he was making $25,000 a year, and when he said he was going to leave, the boss was willing to double it for the following year. Imagine? Walking away from $50,000 a year in 1926 dollars?

He walked away—and started his own tire company out of a little office on Tenth Avenue and had cards printed up:

TIRES, INCORPORATED:
WORLD'S LARGEST DISTRIBUTOR.

The world's largest distributor didn't have a tire to his phony name. In his office he had little models of tires circling ashtrays or set vertically in lacquered plaques advertising Goodyear or Firestone. But the country, he knew, was in greater and greater need of tires. More and more cars in every little town in America, and they all needed tires. So, he took the train out to Dayton and Akron and bought up factory seconds. That's all it took—those deals, and the willingness to sleep on a mattress on his desk because it was too late to go uptown, willingness to grab some sleep on an overnight coach train to save the cost of a room.

"You know how I got where I am?" he'd ask me, again and again. "I worked twenty-five hours a day eight goddamn days a week." He'd take the train town to town or drive town to town and stop in at all the little one-pump gas stations, auto repair shops, and show them pictures and take down payments—enough to cover the cost of the tires—and then he'd send in the orders to the factories. West as far as Chicago, south to Lexington, Kentucky, and all through the Northeast. He wore his Christian name and good conservative clothes. The Stetson, that came a couple of years later. He stayed away from "booze and broads."

A couple of scotches in the evening at Polly's he didn't think of as booze. And Polly Adler was not exactly a "broad." When he was in town and not working in the evening, he went to her apartment—she moved her fancy brothel all around New York —West 50s, West 80s, East 50s—but kept the same telephone number, printed on a card with the logo of a parrot, that was in the pocket of stockbrokers, gangsters, ballplayers, politicians. According to Uncle Lloyd, she made each apartment a home, in good taste, with sofas and tables, warm wood, good liquor—this was Prohibition; people knew they could trust Polly's place. She paid off the cops—though they still bounced her around. And she was fun. Dorothy Parker and Robert Benchley from the Algonquin spent evenings at Polly's. "It was a hell of a place to make business contacts," Uncle Lloyd said.

And Polly Adler, who was, in spite of her razzmatazz, as much a cautious loner as my uncle, "took a shine" to him. Well, I've seen the pictures—Lloyd as a young man. He was gorgeous, chiseled face with sharp nose, nose of a Mohawk more than of a Jew, strong cleft chin like Kirk Douglas. He dressed well, came in alone, wasn't brassy. He never got drunk, never took one of her "girls" to a bedroom. Or so he said, and I believe him. *Contacts*, yes—but he also liked to charm Polly, precisely because she was out of bounds. I think that's it. And here's the funny thing: while Polly Adler was part of sophisticated New York and my uncle was becoming a man about town (I just saw in mind's eye the white silk cravat he wore when he took us out to dinner), they were both Russian Jews. He was born in Chicago, but his father was just off the boat from Odessa; Polly (really Pearl) was born in Russia, came over as a young girl. They'd both come a long way.

By all accounts, Polly brought kindness and good humor along. For my uncle, kindness felt like weakness. He could be generous as hell. He loved being generous, magnanimous, a big shot, loved to spend money on people. But when he felt his control threatened, a rage sprang up. Did the rage come from his father, from his father's belt, that came down on all the boys? But least on Louis. As a kid, my uncle learned to make himself someone too important for a beating. And he succeeded. By fourteen, fifteen, he ran the household.

He saw himself as shepherd of the family. In 1926 Uncle Lloyd brought my father to New York from Chicago ("Got to have somebody I can trust, Chuck.") As a yes-man he could boss around? That's not how Uncle Lloyd saw it. He was being responsible, taking his brother along with him on his rise to glory. As a child, according to my father, Lloyd (Louis) was a "namby-pamby" (my father's word), a "sissy," no athlete; a soft, scared Jewish kid chased by the anti-Semites. My father tells how he and the middle brother Jack protected Louis on the street. Uncle Lloyd must have liked the turn-around, putting his older brother under his thumb. "Of course, you've got to change your name, Chuckie. You're known as my big brother, am I right? Can't have one brother Clayton and the other Cohon, am I right?" My father became Chuck Clayton. Within a year Louis, his sister Ann, and his parents had all become Clayton. Lloyd paid them for the inconvenience.

All the grandiosity! The humiliation and rage and grandiosity came early. Without it, he'd never have made it out of Chicago, surely never bought up a square block of midtown-Manhattan real estate. I'd bet there was someone in Chicago, a mentor, a model of possibilities; I'd love to know. By the time I knew him, he was an angry phony—a charming narcissist. My mother warned me not to get entangled with Lloyd. "Don't let him lead you by the nose the way he's led your father." She begged my father to leave him. They fought about this all the time. "Why do you stay with a man like that? That man has ruined our lives."

Later my father would tell me, "He's a disappointed man, my brother. He's not very happy at home. Frankly, your mother thinks my brother's jealous because he has no kids."

Jealous—of my father? That I couldn't believe. And his home on Park Avenue? To a child it was a little palace, Uncle Lloyd and Aunt Bernadine's, full of mirrors in ornate frames and delicate period furniture that I knew Aunt Bernadine had chosen, as she chose the eighteenth and nineteenth century books that lined a wall of the living room. Real books—Alexander Pope, a first posthumous edition; Hazlitt's essays; Thiers' *History of the French Revolution*. Pretty leather bindings, just décor, never opened. I know that because Aunt Bernadine was interested in clothes and bridge, my mother told me. She was never home. And Uncle Lloyd bragged he never read a "goddamn book." "I know what a great student you are, Jackie, and that's swell. Keep it up. Me, I had to go to work when I was just a little older than you. School of Hard Knocks, you get me? *My book is this city,*" he said, the words resonating like prophetic utterance.

"Well, you sure know the city like a book, it's true all right, Lloyd," my father said. "You own this goddamn city," my father said.

"Cut the crap, Chuck. I own one lousy block is what I own. You get me, Jackie?"

I laughed as I was supposed to, as much in his hands as was my father.

"*But,*" he said hoarsely, with a wicked grin up one side of his cheek, "ain't no saying what I'm *gonna* own at this rate."

Was he like this twenty years before, back when he

knew Polly Adler? He must have been more affable. The caricature on the wall of Leone's, a famous restaurant that started as a speakeasy, shows him grinning above the shoulder of a blonde beauty with comically long cigarette holder. When he retired, he grew more affable again. To me at least. "Cause I got money," he'd say—we're sitting over a whiskey at Trader Vic's, "I'm a 'funny guy,' an 'eccentric.' If I were a poor sonofabitch, they'd call me *crazy*." Then he'd hunker down. "Say, Jackie, did I tell you about the time I was friends with Polly Adler?"

When he was in the city, 1927, Lloyd would get through a long day at work, stop for a bite to eat, and then drop in at Polly's. Early in the evening for her business. And when she wasn't on the phone or talking to customers and women, she'd sit with him and listen and sympathize. "I told her things, you get me, Jackie? Not secrets exactly. Sure as hell not business. I told her what it was like working so hard. Well, she worked just as hard. She did. You think that's not work, running an establishment like that, paying off cops, handling the drunks—the ballplayers and the mobsters? I told her how I got where I was. Polly was a sympathetic lady. And I guess she was soft on me. I guess she was nuts about me. Sometimes I even went to sleep in her room—she was out working the clients, you get me? Time she'd come in, I'd be out of there, back to the grindstone. We became friends."

Was he just a handsome, classy guy, full of power and charm? I don't think so. She was a woman who knew how to listen, and I think he felt safe being vulnerable, telling her how lonely he was in "the rat race," how tough he had to pretend to be. And it moved her. She cared about him. That's my story—but who knows?

I've seen Polly Adler's picture—though it's a picture taken years later, when she'd been through a tough time with the Seabury Commission, with the New York Police Department. She had to spend a month in jail. The *New York Times* has a story on Polly Adler as a prisoner, scrubbing floors. Well, that would have been nothing new; she came from as poor a family as Louis Cohon, got sent to America all by herself at thirteen, worked in factories. In that photo Polly has a sweet, soft round face, big lips, puffy nose and cheeks. She called herself Donald Duck and made fun of how she looked entering a nightclub with some of her tall, gorgeous showgirl whores.

She was no beauty, but she was kind and funny, funny and practical. And Uncle Lloyd liked hanging out with the crowd at Polly's, the rich and the smart and the very, very tough. The ballplayers would win a home game or the gangsters would make a killing off some shipment of whiskey, they'd hang out at Polly's and the women would be busy. Al Capone dropped by, though not when my uncle was around. Polly hated the mobsters, but—she said—"business is business." Uncle Lloyd liked the panache; he'd pal with the guys, playing a man's man. When things got really rough and bric-a-brac started breaking, he'd put on his Stetson and leave the rodeo.

But usually he'd listen to the music. He'd sit with a drinking buddy and when Polly was free, he'd kid with her, he'd talk real estate, listen to her worries about a nasty detective. And a couple of times, when she came in her bedroom next morning, he was still there, and my guess is they smooched a little, and maybe she needed special comforting, maybe the night had gone sour, some jerk beating up on one of her "girls." I'm filling in here, because there must have been something—something before she put it to him—"Why don't we spend next Sunday out at Long Beach?"

Sure, she'd be tired when she drove down, but the drive would be a cinch at that hour on a Sunday morning, and he could take the room the night before. And they could be together and then get some sleep and go down to the beach, and she'd treat him to a big shore dinner before she had to get back.

"I was flattered, Jackie," my uncle told me almost half a century later. "Imagine your old stick-in-the-mud uncle as a fancy-man?"

On cue, like my father, I said, "Ah, that's one thing you never were, Uncle Lloyd—a stick-in-the mud."

"Maybe not. Maybe not. They tell me I was quite the boy," he laughed, barked a big laugh. I winced, but I listened.

"So what happened?"

"Well. . ." He hunkers down over the big table at Trader Vic's and I lean toward his guttural whisper. "So,

I make the reservation, and Saturday night I get down to Long Beach early, sun still up, and I check in and I walk the boardwalk. I remember what I was wearing. I had this gorgeous cream-colored linen suit, it was something. And my two-toned shoes. And I had a goddamn good dinner in me and the Queen of Sex, you get me, from the greatest city in the world, was driving out to have a little rendezvous" (he pronounced it, intentionally, *renn-dayz-vouzzz* in broad Western accent) with the Kid from Chicago. And okay, she was no great beauty, I admit that, but she was a swell lady, Jackie. I kind of felt—" and he tapped his chest. "I felt pretty fabulous that evening. A big shot. I liked the feeling. . . But I was still a little wet behind the ears, those days. No—I *was*. What the hell did I know? Nowadays, Jackie, you don't have to tell me—you're an experienced guy. Every little hippie punk is experienced, you get me? But I didn't get where I was by bumming around. I was in Indiana knocking on gas station doors to get orders. I was taking the boat train to Boston or the train to Chicago and putting together a customer base. This was before we had the big place in New York. Now, I was a stunning guy, I've got to admit it. But I wasn't exactly used to this kind of thing. People believe what they believe. I looked the part. But as the evening went on, see, I grew uneasy. Uncomfortable. I looked at myself in the full-length mirror in the elevator, and you know who I saw? I saw a gangster. In a cream-colored suit. I stuck my hand in my pocket and pretended it was a gun. Lots of laughs. But then I was alone in my big room with the moon up over the great Atlantic Ocean, and I was in silk pajamas, and the windows were open—it was a hot night but a breeze off the ocean helped. And I lay there. And I lay there. And I started to sweat. . . ."

What, he worries, is he getting himself into? Suppose he catches some disease off her? Suppose one of her gangster pals follows her this morning and barges into the room and sprays him with lead and the cream-colored pajamas get drenched in blood and next day his picture is all over the tabloids. Suppose he tries to get away from her and she threatens to let everybody know or gets a tough guy to break his knees. And lying there in the big soft bed in the dark, he says, *I must be crazy. I could lose everything I've worked for.* Lying there in the dark he thinks, *I'm a good Jewish boy, a hard-working Jewish boy and look where I am.*

He said "boy," not "man." He said "*Jewish* boy"—the words letting him hide in an earlier version of himself, one he'd given up even before he became Lloyd Clayton. When he said it to me at Trader Vic's, he had a sentimental quaver in his voice.

"And what happened in the morning? What did you do when she drove out?"

"When she drove out, sonny boy, I wasn't there."

"You weren't there?"

"Before the sun was up, I got my things together, I hustled down to pay off the hotel, and I drove the hell away from Long Beach. We probably passed each other on the road."

"How did you explain it to her? She must have been furious."

Lloyd sat back and folded his arms across his chest. "She must have been. I felt like I'd saved my life."

"You mean you never talked to her again?"

"You're damned right. It was easy. I stayed away from Polly's."

I shook my head. I closed my eyes. I couldn't even pretend to take the story as a joke or a moral victory. It seemed sad to me—more for him than for her. Polly Adler—from what I've read, she could handle rejection. But my uncle—what did the flight from Polly do to him? He stayed away from Polly's place. And next year, he married his cousin Bernadine, and they made each other miserable until she left him—left him because, she told my mother, he "wasn't a *man* for her. You understand me, Jackie?" When my mother told me that, I didn't understand. Now I do.

Scared, scared, Lloyd grew more covered-up, more intensely, solely, the successful businessman. And what about the "good Jewish boy"? No, that he could discard again, no longer useful, leave it behind in the hotel in Long Beach. He was the city sport, who took in the racing season at Saratoga, ordered Tattinger's champagne at the Stork Club. He was the boss who made everyone around him unhappy.

Am I making up the connection between his running away that morning and his becoming a dictator? Would it have been different for him if he'd stayed that morning, if they'd become lovers, at least for a while? Maybe not. Maybe by 1927 his fate was sealed. The stuff it took to get him where he was, it had already done its work. But I like to think of him there in that big sunny hotel room, when the bedraggled Polly comes in, and she says, "What a tough night, Lloyd." And he says, "Well, you come here, little woman, and I'll make it go away." That's the ending I want.

She laughs. And she removes her brash, funny self along with her dress. She's a little squat, not tall and elegant, but she's pretty and she's a little in love with him. And this warm, corrupt, kind-hearted Russian-Jewish woman takes him up on his offer.

TWELVE

Josh

To my wife Sharon,

Was I, a quarter century ago, given a gift, an opening of my soul, so that I might have a way of coping with the death of my eldest son? When I came to Judaism, I had no idea that in a very few years Josh would be sick and in terrible pain, no idea that he'd die of a testicular cancer that had spread through his body, too deep, too far gone, to heal.

Josh was thirty-two when he died.

It's not that prayers soothed my pain. It's been almost twenty years, and still, hardly a day goes by when I don't think of Josh and howl, silently or aloud; howl aloud when no one can hear. But I'm grateful I have my Judaism—my prayers, my study—to give my pain a fuller context.

You, my wife, Sharon, you were the catalyst for my taking on Judaism. About twenty-five years ago, when our son, Aaron, was two or three years old, you said he needed to be part of a community—didn't I think so?—either with me at synagogue or with you at Quaker meeting. All right, I said, I'll give it a try, but you know I don't have any religious faith.

I was a cultural Jew. I'd take part in a Seder on Passover. We'd borrow a sixteen-millimeter projector and watch a scene from *The Ten Commandments,* laugh at Charleston Heston as Moses, holding back the Red Sea. That was it for my Judaism. But after we talked about Aaron's being part of a community, about a religious education, I went to Saturday morning services at the synagogue in Amherst. Impossible! Bored and alienated by the Hebrew that I couldn't read and by the god-awful platitudes when the prayers were in English, I felt like walking out. Maybe I did walk out—I can't remember.

At home the issue was dropped.

Then, some months later, I tried again. I don't remember how often I went to synagogue or when it was that something clicked in me. I know I learned to chant some of the prayers, having only the vaguest idea what they were saying. Then one Saturday morning I was asked by the *gabbai*—a kind of sexton—Will you carry the Torah scroll? Of course I would, though I felt something of an imposter—an actor playing a role.

The scroll holds the five books of Moses. It's not only too precious to touch with the finger, for fear of damaging it; it's too sacred. When you read from the Torah, you use a *yad*—a silver pointer. Then what am I doing holding it?

I remember the heft of it—the heavy scroll on two wooden rollers, covered in a braided fabric and a crown and breastplate of silver—but as I carried the scroll around the synagogue to be touched by everyone—by prayer book or the fringe of a tallit—I felt I was carrying a culture, a people. And maybe because so many had touched the covered scroll, I was connected to the other congregants.

And I found myself in tears. In tears? *This is ridiculous,* I remember thinking. *False sentiment. Stop this.* I couldn't stop. I was carrying thousands of years of a people's faith and a people's pain. I was holding something precious, and I didn't deserve to hold it, but there I was, holding it, carrying it in a procession with the rabbi, the gabbai, and another congregant.

After the scroll had been laid on a slanted desk and the cover removed, after seven members of the congregation had blessed the Torah, and, after each blessing, someone had read a passage from the *parashah* for this week—the same passage of Torah read in synagogues all over the world on this day—the scroll was lifted to show to the congregation, then covered and given to me to carry around the synagogue again. This time I didn't cry. But I felt something had happened to me. There was so much I didn't understand, something so much deeper than me.

After services that day, I walked to the social hall with the rabbi, a woman then in her forties. Sheila Weinberg is important to this story. "I don't know why I felt what I felt," I said to her. She nodded and spoke to me with her hands; she cupped her hands, then held them open, palms up, and stretched them out and nodded and smiled, as if, speaking with her hands, she was telling me she was receiving me, she understood.

"Can I spend a few minutes with you during the week?"

I made an appointment and one afternoon went to her office. "I don't know anything about God," I said. Silence. Then, "I know I don't believe in a *God*." Sheila's hands, palms up, opened as if to say, *who does?* And she smiled and nodded as if to accept what I had said, as if she wanted me to know that she accepted it, that maybe no one believed in the kind of God I didn't believe in, that not to believe wasn't a block. Or maybe she was simply saying with those wonderful hands of hers, waving as if conducting an orchestra, and that generous smile of hers, *I hear what you're saying and it's just where you ought to be for now.*

Because I was a writer and teacher of literature, she suggested books for me. Looking back, I'd say they were simple, beautiful books, essential books—like Buber's *I and Thou* or Heschel's *Sabbath*. But books led to classes, classes led to more books. I studied; I began to deliver a few *divrei Torah*—Torah talks—at Shabbat services. And what about God? Oh, yes: God. The question simply stopped being crucial—stopped being . . . interesting. In some weird way, *God*, whatever that meant, was present; present beyond definition. I suppose you could say that I didn't know what I meant, and that not knowing was all right; what I *meant* didn't *matter*. Theology didn't matter.

What did matter?

My life began to be suffused by my experience of, and my longing for, holiness.

***

My son Josh, he was filled with the spirit that surrounds us, that suffuses us. Josh, a singer-songwriter in his twenties, wrote about people opening to the spirit. We *both* did—I in writing of stories, Josh in his songs. He had become a *bar mitzvah,* but his spiritual nature had little to do with Judaism. Here's the chorus of one of his songs:

> If you want to get through to the other side
> Let the dragonfly come and give you a ride
> Every day you're born and every night you die
> Let the dragonfly come and give you a ride

We used to talk on the phone more than once a week. He opened for a famous singer at very large venues—with voice and acoustic guitar, he performed his own songs.

And then, he informed us, casually—like it was no big deal—that he was in pain. His back hurt. And then he began to lose weight. He didn't much believe in "Western medicine." He went to an acupuncturist-herbalist and didn't go to a doctor for tests. And then, when a strong painkiller didn't help, he spoke to the woman he rented an apartment from, a doctor who practiced at UCLA

Medical, and she examined him and saw right away something was terribly wrong. She drove him to the hospital—but too late, too late.

I flew to L.A. to see him. The plane was delayed—winter weather—and by the time I got to the hospital, they'd just begun to induce a coma to save his strength. Josh was getting bleary, but still smiling his sweet, generous smile. "Hi, Pop. Pop? I'm not going to die, am I?" "No, no, of course not."

We sat by his bedside in the ICU. His mother wouldn't let me say blessings in Hebrew for his recovery—she associated the Hebrew language with prayers for the dead, and that terrified her. I had to go outside into the hall to pray for a *refuah sheleima*—a complete healing. Josh's friends and family took turns by his bed. He entered the hospital on December 12th; he died, never having awoken, on January 19th, 2000

So many people loved him. So many. The next day—on such little notice—hundreds attended his funeral and burial in L.A. His mother was so broken that she couldn't be present. Later she had gold rings made for those who'd sat by his bed in the hospital. "A circle of Josh" she had inscribed on the inside of the ring. My daughter Laura worked hard the next months, the next years, to keep Josh's music alive. Almost twenty years later she's still doing it. She was helped by her husband and by friends who established, and have maintained, for two decades, Josh's website.

The question with which I began: Did I find Judaism; was I given access to that path, so that I might be able to get through this terrible time?

I don't think it helped in easing suffering. In fact, my Judaism deepened my suffering; let it express more—more fully. It let me dig into grief, not push it away.

You asked me to go to the synagogue in order to bring Aaron into a community. We wanted to create a context for Aaron's religious education. It turns out I was the one who needed a religious education.

There's a story of the Buddha. A woman, holding a dead infant, comes to the Buddha and asks, "My child has died. How can I bring him back to life?" And the Buddha says, "Go into the village from door to door and from the family that has not lost anyone take four mustard seeds." And of course, she can't find such a family; every family had known loss. And so, she buries her child and, deepened in understanding, returns to the Buddha.

Back in Amherst we sat *Shiva*—meaning *seven*—the prescribed number of days for sitting at home and mourning. Traditionally the mirrors are covered, and mourners sit on cushions. I didn't know the rules. People came and went. Congregants I knew, even those I didn't know, came and brought food and we held a brief service, another service. I told stories about Josh; I played Josh's music. I displayed his photographs.

I let my beard grow. According to tradition, a man lets his beard grow for a month or until it's commented on. You, Sharon, didn't comment for a month or two—until Rabbi Weinberger pulled you aside and said, "You might comment now. Ask him to shave." And so, I shaved.

After days of sitting and mourning I tried to say prayers for Josh's soul and whenever I could, I attended *minyanim*—services of at least ten adult Jews, a community, able to say the Mourner's Kaddish. I felt I should accept—accept our loss, felt that it was a disgrace to mix bitterness with my grief. But I couldn't accept. I spoke to the Chabad rabbi. He asked me, "Suppose you could speak to Hashem [God]. What could Hashem say that you'd accept?"

"Nothing. Not a thing."

"Exactly. Nothing. So, it's a mystery. Unsolvable. Do you accept the mystery?"

"What choice do I have?"

"Exactly."

I remember Josh's last visit, not long before he became sick. He taught me some qi gung forms, exercises to lift and balance energy. We spoke about the spirit that expresses itself through us and through all things. We meditated together. He played his new songs on a cassette recorder. He'd spent days, he told us, visiting a friend whose wife had died. Orthodox Jews came and chanted psalms.

We spoke about negative energy. He remembered times I used to get angry. I remembered, too. "It was as if you took poison into your own body," he said. It's true.

"We also had good times"—I reminded him—"times that filled us both with positive energy. With light." He agreed. He showed me how to drain negative energy out of our bodies into a tree, touching our fingers to the trunk.

He mentioned that he was in a little pain. I think I gave him a pill.

Saturday morning—this was a few months before he died—we went to synagogue together. I was given an *Aliyah*—I came up to the *bima* to offer a blessing over the Torah. Somehow, I blanked out the melody, though I'd made this blessing before and had remembered the melody—maybe because I so wanted to show Josh I could chant musically. It didn't matter. We grinned at each other; we hugged.

Remember, Sharon, his calls on the telephone, maybe from a city where he knew no one, remember the "hey-hey-hey-hey announcing him, remember he'd speak to one of us, describing the city and the awful restaurants and something funny that went down at last night's show. He'd speak to me, he'd speak to you, ask about our work. Sometimes I'd meet him in Cambridge—his mother and stepfather lived nearby in Brighton—and once we skated together on rollerblades along the Charles.

I felt so satisfied with what he'd become, what he was becoming.

Josh is gone and not gone. It's hard not just to bear his going but, even two decades on, to believe it. On each anniversary of his death—his *yahrzeit*, year-time—I light a memorial candle and within a *minyan* I say Mourners' Kaddish.

If on a Shabbat I carry the Torah scroll up and down the aisle in the sanctuary, I feel in its weight my son, the loss of my son. If I chant a blessing, I feel Josh's spirit; feel a connection between my lost son and the scroll.

I don't expect to meet Josh's soul in any kind of heaven. But at times in an ordinary day, I stop and feel his presence, whether from inside myself or from his spirit—his spirit loose in the world and beyond, riding his dragonfly.

Thirteen

A Broken Compass

IN THE DREAM, my repeated night dream, I'm anxious, uneasy. I'm supposed to drive somewhere. But the roads are unfamiliar. No, not exactly unfamiliar. I've seen these roads before, but I've forgotten where they lead. I turn on the engine of the car and play with the electronics to bring up a compass on the screen. But there's interference. When I find the compass, the needle swings wildly from direction to direction. Which way is north? Somehow, magically, I pluck the virtual compass from the screen—an image—into my hand. My dream hand.

And so now, in the dream, it's become a physical compass. But the needle still spins. Maybe it's distorted by the heavy body of the car—the metal of the car disorienting the compass. I step away from the car, but the needle still waves erratically. *Non compass mentis.* Turning back, I don't see the car. It's gone. It's slipped away—down the hill—driving without a driver, away, away. I should go after it, but I don't. I'll have to walk.

There are several roads, but I'm not such a fool as to take one.

I don't even know where I need to go. Or why.

Now in the dream I suddenly realize that you, my wife, you've been with me all this time. I'm supposed to bring you home. I know a shortcut, through a parking lot at the university—from parking lot to parking lot. But I am unable to find my shortcut. I try to explain. I'm upset and I apologize. You don't seem upset. I have no car. But I have the keys. I have the keys and no car. How will I bring you home?

Compass and *keys, roads* taken or not taken. It's embarrassing—that it's so obvious. But I'm not playing with symbols. They're playing with me. The dream varies, night after night. Maybe it varies so as not to bore me. In some dreams I'm driving home alone, and now I know the right road. But the road is blocked by a fallen tree. Or there are two roads. One looks right—a shortcut I've taken often—but it leads me in the wrong direction. I'm left in anxiety. Butterflies flutter in my stomach. I see no way to get home.

And then, somehow, I *am* home—I've gotten home, and it's worse. My own children don't speak to me. You, Sharon, turn from me. Besides, it's the wrong house. A vacation rental. We—you and I, family and friends—need to find a local restaurant because our pots and pans have been put away for our move. I try to convince my family and friends that there are good restaurants right nearby with plenty of room, tables empty, but they're not interested. No one listens to me. Let's go to the beach, I say. I feel I should have suggested that long ago. Here it is the end of vacation and we've lost the chance.

***

These dreams, I suppose they're telling me I'm lost, blocked off from a new direction for my life—my life with Parkinson's. The dreams are asking a question, posing a riddle. And the thing is, I already know the answer: I don't have to choose to do anything, not a thing, don't have to find a direction, don't have to find the right road, and why do I need to feed the others?

Tell that to my dreamer.

***

Lifting out of sleep, in the dawn or in the day from a Parkinson nap, a brief sleep of exhaustion, I hear baritone voices, voices of a pair of newscasters, or at times women in a higher register. I can tell myself all day that it's just the whisper of blood in my ears, but I know they're speaking—speaking just beyond my understanding.

Remember, Sharon, when I was almost falling asleep last week—me in eye mask, you reading next to me in bed—and I asked you to *shh,* turn down the music on your iPad—those singers, women singing over a band? *What* music, there is no music, go back to sleep, you whispered. Oh, my sweet wife, you never expected to be married to someone so peculiar.

I dream I've agreed to teach at the university again—a creative writing workshop and a class in literature. I'm not prepared. I go into a classroom and find about twenty students waiting for me. I know, somehow, that most of them want to write poetry, but I don't *do* poetry, and I suggest an exercise in fiction.

Now I have to leave early, fearing they'll discover I'm a fraud—and besides, I have to urinate. I hurry from the classroom to a room where students are milling about, and I *do* urinate—into a paper cup, but I'm holding the cup upside down, and urine spills over the table. Students kindly take off the tablecloth and reassure me. Now I go to my literature class asking myself which books to tell them to read. But there's no one there.

***

Last night, you caught me just before I fell out of bed in the middle of a dream. This morning I told you the dream: I'm standing with my son, on the street of a broken-down city. An old Volvo station wagon, like one I used to own in the seventies, comes barreling down the street, and as it passes, too close, I curse the driver. He turns back, furious, and comes at me. The first pass was accident—careless driving; the second, intention. He didn't hit me, but he caught me with his car; I was outside the Volvo, attached somehow to the passenger door, dragged along the street. I had almost gotten away when you shook me and held me back from falling to the floor. "Just a dream," you said. "You had a dream. Go back to sleep."

"Sorry, sorry."

You catch me as I fall.

You are my compass; you are my lodestone. Especially now, when, in my damaged state, I can't always tell where to go or how to get there. Just so you know: I'm grateful.

Oh, if I were to say this to you, I know what you'd say: that *I* am also *your* compass. And we know that beyond us or deep within us there is something holy, something true, that orients us both. Family?—yes, and something beyond family. We dance our dance, circling each other—circling north and south to the music.

***

Mornings, we sit down to work, each of us alone at laptops, me in my study, you in yours. We know how lucky we are to have this beautiful space, lucky to live in this quiet place where we spend our summers. I begin with exercises and morning prayers—then try to write.

You, you're writing a book about our place—about Bound Brook Island in Wellfleet on Cape Cod, no longer, but once, an island—writing a kind of micro-history of a small piece of land, a history going forward from the last ice age to the present day. You hold up your magnifying glass to census records, trace family trees, write about the interwoven families who lived here and about the diminishment of those families on the island—the depopulation of Bound Brook Island. It's like a micro-history of the world.

And me, I'm writing about disorientation, about getting lost, or fearing I'll be lost, a ghost of myself, a dizzy ghost, woozy ghost, and about the dreams and the voices that come to me at the edge of waking.

Paradoxically, writing about disorientation helps orient me.

We meet for lunch. We don't speak much about our morning adventures building word upon word—building, replacing, erasing, rebuilding. Usually, we talk about the children, about the house, about books we're reading, plans for the afternoon. Sometimes I don't feel much like speaking. I'm too exhausted, too ragged, ol' Parkinson's got me. I can barely wait to finish lunch so I can lie down for my nap. I don't say much. I go dumb.

I'm a decade older than you. I wonder what it will be like for you when I'm gone. We don't talk about that, but listen, I am in my mid-eighties. And though Parkinson's doesn't kill, it weighs you down so something else can kill you.

Oh, it'll be all right. You're very strong, you'll have good friends and loving, grown children—one, Aaron, from our marriage and two, Sasha and Laura, from my previous marriages—and their mates and children. All, in the heart, one family—for both of us, our magnetic north.

We enjoy telling friends how we met. A mutual friend, a writer, waited until she felt I was ready to meet you, enough of my grief of separation worn away. "I have a friend who edits a literary magazine, *Agni*. You might send Sharon a story. Oh—and when you get to Cambridge to see Josh, you might like to meet her."

We met over lunch in Cambridge, and in a couple of weeks we had dinner at a restaurant halfway between Cambridge and Amherst. Then, after a while, you met my children and my first wife, by then a good friend, and, later, met my second wife, now a good friend. And I read your magazine. And you took my story—and took me along with it.

We began to live together as much as we could while being two hours apart. Some weekends we spent in Cambridge, some in the house I built—helped build—near Amherst. And all it took to love one another, to love and be really married and put aside our foolish defenses, was a mere ten years or more and raising our child together, and becoming a family, and suffering together when Josh died and when my first wife died.

How long have we been together now, you and I? For more than thirty-five years.

We spent so many Thanksgivings together, you and me and my previous wives and their husbands. And our children, adult children. I remember Thanksgivings before Josh died and before his mother, Marilyn, died. I remember you and my two ex-wives pulling chairs together after Thanksgiving dinner. Talking, laughing. Passing by on my way to the kitchen, I felt proud of our combined family. I still feel proud of us, grateful for our ties.

But the dreams I've been having, oh, these recent dreams, tell me something entirely different, tell me I can't find my way home, or tell me that at home I'm not completely at home. Our lovely, composed, almost comic modern family—wives knowing each other as loving friends, husbands and grown children all joined and enjoying each other—the family I love—becomes something I'm not completely a part of. I love and I'm loved, but I'm also apart, I'm lost, a Parkinson's ghost. When I leave—leave altogether—as the family misses Josh and misses Marilyn, I'm sure it will miss me. I know, Sharon, that you'll miss me. But already I'm not all here. I'm halfway between Josh, my beautiful son, gone for two decades now, and my living family.

Fourteen

Coda: A Mystery

For a long time now, more than half a century, I've been courting with my words a mystery just beyond my grasp. *Courting, fishing*: metaphors of desire, of longing. I've sent my line into deep water, not expecting to catch anything. The line has no hook at the end; my words have been a way of connecting, or trying to connect, to what's down there, a wire carrying a signal. A pulse . . . an answering pulse?

If I breathe in, taking a long breath, I can sense a presence. I can call it the sacred; I can call it God. Best not give it a name. Best to say, simply, *I love*—but not name the Beloved. If I look into your eyes, beloved, I am in touch with the longed-for, or, rather, with the longing itself. Isn't that enough?

If I look out at the rock outcropping by the house, ancient rock, left here at the retreat of the last ice age, I know its solidity is an illusion. The longed-for, the imagined, is real—real beneath, or through, or within, the visible and palpable. Energy has taken shape, has tricked us into believing that the shape is the whole deal, ultimate reality—when it's not. It's like color printing made in circles of dots, rosettes with dots of different saturations of color. The image is an illusion, composed in the eye.

Who am *I* then? A wind could go through me. Voices come to me as I wake. I don't catch their drift. Are they part of me? If they are, so is the sough of wind in trees, or the sound of waves when the wind comes from the bay in the west.

These aren't voices in dreams. Voices in dreams make sense or nonsense but sometimes I remember the words. The voices I mean, yes, maybe due to my Parkinson's, are dialogues overheard from another room. If I don't understand the voices, it's all right. If they're just a neurological buzzing in my head, it's all right. Are they simply the rhythm the heart makes, a thumping in my inner ear? What matters is that the sounds link me to the essential, complex rhythms in the world—link me to the mystery.

And the rhythms of my sentences, *these* sentences—they try to evoke, as best they can, the real, beneath the palpable and visible—try to coax the holy out of the depths, out of the connection between words. But it's not just words. Once, and not on a magic pill, after meditating for well over an hour and then resting, I felt my soul lift out of my body and hover above me. The perceiving eye, or "I," was looking down at my body; it frightened me, and at once I dropped back into myself.

I am not contained between my hat and boots. Nor am I separate from the tree outside my window. The window both separates and connects us, and the tree, the tree is connected to the earth. I'm not postulating; not postulant or apostle, laying out a postulate. I'm simply here inside you or part of you, never wholly apart.

Then, when I die, how can I wholly disappear?

So hard to put this experience into words. It's not just the living trees or the living creatures—they're not the only ones whose spirit remains in dialogue with me, but created things, too—the wood desk on which my laptop rests, the laptop itself. Photos in my study of my long-gone grandparents from Odessa or Kishinev. It's as if I'm being spoken to; I know it's only me, imagining. Still, it feels true—feels like the truth.

My grandparents speak from their frames. Studio portraits of each family to send back home to Odessa, to a little town near Kishinev. And pictures of myself speak to me— pictures from thirty, forty, fifty years ago. My old selves, there on the wall. I let my old, gone selves address me. I'm not ashamed of them. I feel affection and even respect for the poor fool there on the wall. He's smiling, trying to please, trying to appear strong—though we both know how incomplete he is, the young man in those pictures.

And my father addresses me, in a photo from when he was maybe thirteen, the oldest of three brothers. He's in the middle, hands on the shoulder of a brother, the uncle I met only once. I see deep kindness in my father's eyes. He's not the frightened, angry father I knew. But the youngest of the three brothers, Lloyd, who became the rich brother—who became my father's boss—already wears a tough-kid sneer and stands slightly apart, challenges the photographer, doesn't touch my father.

My mother, framed, is there on the wall as a beautiful adolescent—she claimed to have been voted Miss Rochester—as a woman in her seventies, as an elegant young woman in a color-tinted photograph made toward the end of the 1920's. I'm sad for her, knowing her future, now past, that she won't have the life she hopes for, won't marry a wealthy man, won't become a fabulous New York doyenne. She'll marry and live in bitterness and blame her life on my father.

Most of the pictures on that wall of my study are of Josh. My sweet dead son, so present in this room. Longing connects us; we speak to each other. *I guess I'm dead, Pop. I guess this is what you call death. But we can still talk together. Can't we?*

In one picture, a poster of his tour as a singer-songwriter, he's looking down past the guitar on his lap—maybe at his music stand, but that's not in the picture. At his feet his dog, Kaya, looks at the camera. The guitar seems to move. Of course. Stare at anything long enough and it begins to move. Josh is playing and singing in the mode of silence. I listen in the mode of loving memory.

Of course, there is no speech between us. No speech,

no music, audible, inaudible. What connects us is absence. I send my line down and down into that absence, not expecting miracles. It's enough to feel the longing. Longing links us. Separation links us: a paradox.

Suffering comes from desire. Longing, while part of the real, distorts the real. Love expresses the real.

Waking, before you, beside you, I whisper into the mystery, *Modeh ani lefenecha. . . .* I give thanks before You, King, living and eternal, you have returned my soul within me, great is Your faithfulness.

I *am* thankful, I have enough, I have plenty. There's you, beloved, and my living children and my grandchildren. There's this house, there's the green and the flowering outside my window. Shouldn't I be thankful?

But I'm not telling my truth: Though I want to be thankful, I'm aware instead of my exhaustion from Parkinson's. Here I am, Lord, stumbling to the bathroom, and though I've slept deeply, my body is ragged and full of sleep; or here I am, sitting at my desk, struggling to put sentences together.

Still, I feel close to the truth beyond desire, beyond the words I can't quite hear. The mystery. I'll be gone soon into the mystery. The joke about Parkinson's: you don't die from Parkinson's, you have to live with it—you die from something else. And then? That's the mystery. I'll remain in the mystery, in memory, and in the words.